The Literary Agenda

The Necessity of Young Adult Fiction

DEBORAH LINDSAY WILLIAMS

OXFORD
UNIVERSITY PRESS

OXFORD
UNIVERSITY PRESS

Great Clarendon Street, Oxford, OX2 6DP,
United Kingdom

Oxford University Press is a department of the University of Oxford.
It furthers the University's objective of excellence in research, scholarship,
and education by publishing worldwide. Oxford is a registered trade mark of
Oxford University Press in the UK and in certain other countries

Published in the United States of America by Oxford University Press
198 Madison Avenue, New York, NY 10016, United States of America

British Library Cataloguing in Publication Data
Data available

Library of Congress Control Number: 2022945380

ISBN 978–0–19–284897–0

DOI: 10.1093/oso/9780192848970.001.0001

Printed by Integrated Books International, United States of America

Series Introduction

The Crisis in, the Threat to, the Plight of the Humanities: enter these phrases in Google's search engine and there are twenty-three million results, in a great fifty-year-long cry of distress, outrage, fear, and melancholy. Grant, even, that every single anxiety and complaint in that catalog of woe is fully justified—the lack of public support for the arts, the cutbacks in government funding for the humanities, the imminent transformation of a literary and verbal culture by visual/virtual/digital media, the decline of reading ... And still, though it were all true, and just because it might be, there would remain the problem of the response itself. Too often there's recourse to the shrill moan of offended piety or a defeatist withdrawal into professionalism.

The Literary Agenda is a series of short polemical monographs that believes there is a great deal that needs to be said about the state of literary education inside schools and universities and more fundamentally about the importance of literature and of reading in the wider world. The category of "the literary" has always been contentious. What *is* clear, however, is that increasingly it is dismissed or unrecognized as a way of thinking or an arena for thought. It is skeptically challenged from within, for example, by the sometimes rival claims of cultural history, contextualized explanation, or media studies. It is shaken from without by even greater pressures: by economic exigency and the severe social attitudes that can follow from it; by technological change that may leave the traditional forms of serious human communication looking merely antiquated. For just these reasons, this is the right time for renewal, to start reinvigorated work into the meaning and value of literary reading for the sake of the future.

It is certainly no time to retreat within institutional walls. For all the academic resistance to "instrumentalism," to governmental measurements of public impact and practical utility, literature exists in and across society. The "literary" is not pure or specialized or self-confined; it is not restricted to the practitioner in writing or the academic in studying. It exists in the whole range of the world which is its subject matter: It consists in what non-writers actively receive from

writings when, for example, they start to see the world more imaginatively as a result of reading novels and begin to think more carefully
about human personality. It comes from literature making available
much of human life that would not otherwise be existent to thought or
recognizable as knowledge. If it is true that involvement in literature,
so far from being a minority aesthetic, represents a significant contri-
bution to the life of human thought, then that idea has to be argued
at the public level without succumbing to a hollow rhetoric or bow-
ing to a reductive world-view. Hence the effort of this series to take its
place *between* literature and the world. The double-sided commitment
to occupying that place and establishing its reality is the only "agenda"
here, without further prescription as to what should then be thought
or done within it.

What is at stake is not simply some defensive or apologetic "justi-
fication" in the abstract. The case as to why literature matters in the
world not only has to be argued conceptually and strongly tested by
thought, but it should be given presence, performed and brought to
life in the way that literature itself does. That is why this series includes the writers themselves, the novelists and poets, in order to try
to close the gap between the thinking of the artists and the thinking
of those who read and study them. It is why it also involves other
kinds of thinkers—the philosopher, the theologian, the psychologist,
the neuroscientist—examining the role of literature within their own
life's work and thought, and the effect of that work, in turn, upon
literary thinking. This series admits and encourages personal voices
in an unpredictable variety of individual approaches and expressions,
speaking wherever possible across countries and disciplines and tem-
peraments. It aims for something more than intellectual assent: rather
the literary sense of what it is like to feel the thought, to embody an
idea in a person, to bring it to being in a narrative or in aid of adven-
turous reflection. If the artists refer to their own works, if other thinkers
return to ideas that have marked much of their working life, that is not
their vanity nor a failure of originality. It is what the series has asked
of them: to speak out of what they know and care about, in whatever
language can best serve their most serious thinking, and without the
necessity of trying to cover every issue or meet every objection in each
volume.

Philip Davis

Acknowledgments

A long time ago, when I worked at Iona College, a group of students begged me to "teach a *Harry Potter* class." It was long enough ago, in fact, that J. K. Rowling hadn't even finished the series, much less become infamous for her remarks about trans people. Putting together that course, and listening to the way the students engaged with Harry and the other young adult books on the syllabus, marked the beginning of my scholarly interest in YA literature.

My thinking about YA literature intersected with my thinking about cosmopolitanism when I started teaching at NYU Abu Dhabi (NYUAD), a four-year liberal arts university with students who come from almost every country in the world. The *Harry Potter* course became "Myth, Magic, and Representations of Childhood," and the conversations that occurred over the decade that I taught that course have shaped the ideas that are at the core of this book. I am grateful to all the students who have shared their insights with me—and although a full list is beyond the scope of these pages, I want to make sure to mention Aishah Shafiq, Zoe Patterson, Dominique Lear, Nikolaj Nielsen, Amrita Anand, Malak Abdel-Ghaffar, Rabha Ashry, Gabrielle Flores, Viviana Kawas, and Jamie Sutherland.

Toshi Reagon, singer, songwriter, and activist, composed a musical version of *Parable of the Sower* that I first saw in a workshop version at The Arts Center at NYUAD. The music and Toshi's commitment to the legacy of Octavia E. Butler forever changed the way I thought about the novel. I feel unbelievably lucky to have been able to hear the work performed several times and to have talked with Toshi about the ongoing project; I owe Bill Bragin a debt of thanks for bringing Toshi's work to my attention.

Early work on *Akata Witch* and *Trail of Lightning* was presented at "Being Human in YA Literatures" at the University of Roehampton in London, and later appeared as an article in the inaugural issue of the *International Journal of Young Adult Literature* (*IJYAL*). The anonymous reviewers for the journal asked incredibly useful and thoughtful questions and I am grateful for their insights. I am also grateful to Emily

Corbett and Alison Waller, the conference co-conveners and founders of *IJYAL*, whose generosity and scholarship have so enriched the field of YA studies.

At Oxford University Press, Jacqueline Norton shepherded this proposal through the review process—a task made significantly more challenging because of the pandemic. I am grateful to Aimee Wright and Eleanor Collins for seeing the manuscript through production and to Philip Davis for seeing that a discussion of young adult literature fit into the Literary Agenda series.

The proposal for this book, and much of the manuscript, was written during the early years of the pandemic. During that dark time, when the world was sealed off from itself, I was lucky enough to be in conversation with some of my marvelous colleagues at NYUAD: the "Pod"—Shamoon Zamir, Marzia Balzani, Matty Silverstein, and Roberta Wertman. Scholarship alone cannot sustain us: we need friendship, laughter, and the occasional stiff drink to thrive. The Pod has provided all of these things, and more. I am grateful to Justin Stearns and Nathalie Peutz for the many impromptu and thought-provoking conversations about climate change, YA fiction, and teaching. A debt also to Shireen RK Patell, who read and commented on an early version of this manuscript. My decades-long conversation with Marion Wrenn about writing, teaching, and life have helped shaped my thinking about this book–and everything else.

I am writing these acknowledgments in the sad aftermath of my colleague Ken Nielsen's sudden and untimely death, and it is to him that I owe a profound debt. His incisive wit and compassionate intelligence, as well as his fierce devotion to queer and marginalized people, create a formidable legacy, one that I strive to honor every time I step into a classroom or talk with a student. His friendship remains one of the great gifts of my life.

There must also be thanks given to my family, who made sure I felt their love across the many time zones that separated the U.S. and Abu Dhabi, where I was living while I wrote this book.

And finally, an utterly inadequate thank you to my husband, Cyrus R. K. Patell, index-maker extraordinaire, whose belief in me knows no bounds and whose thoughtful comments improved every page of this book. I could not ask for a better partner in scholarship or in life.

My sons, Liam and Caleb, are now themselves young adults, launching themselves into this uncertain and complicated world. This book is dedicated to them, in love and hope.

Contents

Introduction: Why "Kids' Books?"

"No wonder your course is so popular," said a colleague. "It's a course on *kids' books*." His voice dripped with disdain. He didn't come right out and call me a panderer, but it was implied: Kids' lit, in his mind, was not a serious endeavor and *certainly* not a subject for university students. The class is actually about young adult literature, but to my colleague it's all the same thing, and neither is an appropriate subject for college students. As is often the case when someone says something ungenerous, I didn't have a ready response. What I wish I'd said is that he should be glad that I'm teaching these books because without "kids' books," there'd be no readers; and without readers, there'd be no writers, and probably far fewer students with an interest in the "serious" adult books that he teaches.

My colleague's dismissive comment is not unusual, despite the steady rise in children's literature as a focus of scholarship. There are numerous refereed journals, professional organizations, and academic publishers with children's literature imprints; scores of dissertations are written every year in the United States and the United Kingdom that center on some aspect of children's literature (including in the fields of library science, education and pedagogy, publishing, and marketing). And yet somehow "children's literature" is seen as peripheral, not as important as literature written for grown-ups, even though children's literature is the only category of literature that can accurately be described as universal: We have all of us been children and teenagers, which means we have all been, at some point, the target audience for these books. As teenagers, when we find ourselves in books, it seems to resonate more powerfully than when we have those flickers of recognition in our adult reading. A student of mine who grew up between Seoul and Los Angeles found that resonance in Nnedi Okorafor's *Akata Witch* (2011), which is about a Nigerian girl who grows up in New York and is teased for her accent, and then moves to Aba, in Nigeria, where she is also teased for her accent. "That's *me*," said the student with great joy. "I didn't talk the right way no matter where I was—and so I kinda stopped talking in public for a while." Children's literature, like all reading, helps us to connect with ourselves, to deepen our understanding of our own experiences—and it also establishes connections across difference that we might not otherwise expect, in part because we are conditioned to think more about difference than we are about connection. Why would we imagine, for example, that a Korean college kid would identify with a Nigerian "tween"?

Talking about "children's literature" sets up several problems of definition, not the least of which is the question of "category." Children's literature encompasses all genres and forms: picture books, chapter books for early readers, young adult (YA) books; speculative fiction and nonfiction and science fiction and queer romance and tragedy, thrillers and comedies and cookbooks. In this Literary Agendas book, I am going to focus on YA fiction, which in general terms is often thought to have emerged with S. E. Hinton's novel *The Outsiders*, published in 1967, when Hinton was herself eighteen. The book focuses on the conflict between two groups of teenagers—the "greasers" and the "socs" (Socials)—and is narrated by Ponyboy Curtis, a greaser and an orphan who lives with his two older brothers. Ponyboy's social and emotional struggles became paradigmatic for the first wave of YA fiction, which purported to be realistic portrayals of tensions that had long been brewing in US society.[1] This novel also popularized the image of the misfit on the margins—Ponyboy is a less privileged and cynical version of Holden Caulfield, the hero of Salinger's *The Catcher in the Rye* (1951). Salinger's book was originally intended for adult readers and became more of a "teen classic" in the aftermath of *The Outsiders* and others. In the first decades after Hinton's novel, the category of "YA" primarily designated fiction that focused on characters between the ages of twelve and eighteen. As Michael Cart points out in a 2008 essay for the Young Adult Library Services Association (YALSA),

> between 1990 and 2000 the number of persons between 12 and 19 soared to 32 million, a growth rate of seventeen percent that significantly outpaced the growth of the rest of the population. The size of this population segment has also increased as the conventional definition of "young adult" has expanded to

include those as young as ten and, since the late 1990s, as old as twenty-five.

(2008 np)

Cart, who has been a long-time advocate for YA literature, also notes that YA now spans all genres and forms.

Further blurring the category of YA is the fact that the readership is often more "A" than "Y." Perhaps freed by the popularity of the *Harry Potter* series, adults are eager consumers of what is considered YA fiction. Rachel Falconer uses the term "crossover fiction" to describe this mixed readership, which she suggests we see as an indication that "children's literature has never existed in a truly separate sphere . . . [because] an essential feature of this category of fiction is that its boundaries are unfixed" (9). Those unfixed boundaries may explain why *Harry Potter and the Deathly Hallows* (2007), had bigger sales for the adult editions than for the children's editions (Falconer 16). Adults, it would seem, not only do most of the writing of YA, but they are also involved at the business end of the publishing process, and at the purchasing end, buying for themselves almost as frequently as they buy for the teenaged readers in their lives. I imagine that adults will be the readers of this book, a fact that further illustrates the blurriness of categorization. Even if adults aren't reading YA for their own pleasure, they are intimately involved in its production.

Unlike, for example, "detective fiction," "YA literature" is at once a designation of content and audience—an audience that is always in the midst of transforming. We have all been teenagers; we have not all been detectives. We can remember ourselves as teenaged readers, the utter immersion with which we used to sink into a story, an experience that hovers, ghost-like, when or if we return to those books as adults. The books become a mirror not only of the moment when they were written but also of where and who we were when we first read them. Because we read these books when we are young (or younger than you are now, presumably, as you read this book), our reading experiences are often more intense, unmediated. The reading is not necessarily "innocent," but it may be, perhaps, unaware of the book's reviews or the author's politics. Philip Pullman suggests that young readers are an exacting audience, even if they might not be "sophisticated" in an adult sense: "in a book for children you can't put the plot on hold

while you posture artistically .... [These readers] have more important things in mind than your dazzling skill" (qtd. in Falconer 5). When
teenagers engage with fiction (unless they're reading a book for school
and thus probably for some kind of an exam, which we might think
of as "transactional reading"– reading for a purpose and information
rather than pleasure), they can be thought of as "lay readers," people
whose reading "proffers the possibility of reconnecting with the every-
day life of literary engagement" (Buurma and Heffernan 115). Unlike
literary scholars—scholars writing for other scholars—for whom the
stereotype of a hermetically sealed discourse is often all too accurate,
teenagers see themselves and their worlds in the texts; their reading
becomes, as Eric Shouse describes it, "a non-conscious experience of
intensity . . . of unformed and unstructured potential" (Shouse qtd. in
Anker and Felski 175). I want to focus on the word "potential" here,
because that's one of the key factors that makes YA literature so important: The readership of YA is one of *potential*. These are readers who
do not yet hold any of the official levers of power and who exist, in a
sense, on the margins of their societies by reason of their age. Many of
them are additionally marginalized by reason of sexuality, ethnicity,
nationality, economics, or religion. What I see in YA literature are the
ways that the texts render the experience of being sidelined and then
offer examples of how readers might imagine themselves as people
with agency in the world. We see characters who discover the ability
to engage with and sometimes even improve the worlds in which they
live. I suppose some would say that it is naïve to think that fiction can
change the world, and perhaps that's true. But people can change the
world—and books can change people.

Fiction allows us to inhabit lives that are not our own: When we
read, we are inside lives and consciousnesses that may be quite different from our daily experiences. As we read, we do not erase differences
between ourselves and the protagonists; instead, we find moments of
connection and resonance that enable us to bridge those differences,
like my Korean American student did in reading *Akata Witch*. Reading
about Sunny Nwazue's experiences on the margins gave the student
insight and language with which to think about her own life: Connections were established across difference. Although she didn't name
it as such, the student had engaged with what I will be calling in this
book a cosmopolitan reading practice, which necessitates a willingness

to engage, to move away from what is comfortable or familiar. Fiction, as the American philosopher Martha Nussbaum says, is what develops "the compassionate imagination, which can make other people's lives more than distant abstractions" (np). It is in abstraction that the threatening Other—the migrant, immigrant, slave—becomes a monster. In *Monster Theory: Reading Culture* (1996), Jeffrey Jerome Cohen stipulates that "the monster's body quite literally incorporates fear, desire, anxiety, and fantasy (ataractic or incendiary), giving them life and an uncanny independence. The monstrous body is pure culture" (4). The monstrous body is a site of ambivalence, in other words, and as such provides the opportunity for negotiation and innovation. In all the novels that I discuss in this book, monsters are at the center, as is the importance of finding different ways of engaging with the monster. What we see, ultimately, is that the very definition of "monster" is being challenged: The monster becomes less about Otherness and more about those individuals and entities that see the planet and its inhabitants solely as commodities. Once we know how to see them, these monsters of commodification—the monsters that threaten the health of the planet—can be found across genres, and not only in the speculative fictions that I discuss here.

This process of engagement is essential to cosmopolitanism, a word that is never used in these novels but is illustrated by them nonetheless. Cosmopolitanism is a term that has been much theorized over the past few decades, although very rarely in the context of children's literature. I want to stress that cosmopolitanism as I see it is a *practice*, something that one does—in reading, in conversation, in the classroom.[2] Originally developed as a response to nationalism, cosmopolitanism offered models for thinking about a global conception of citizenship and in its simplest iteration sees difference as an opportunity rather than a threat. Cosmopolitanism asks us to consider our obligation to others, beyond the ties of family or state. In his seminal book *Cosmopolitanism* (2006), Kwame Anthony Appiah points out that

> people are different, the cosmopolitan knows, and there is much to learn from our differences. Because there are so many human possibilities worth exploring, we neither expect nor desire that every person or every society should converge on a single mode

of life. Whatever our obligations are to others (or theirs to us)
they often have the right to go their own way.

(xv)

It is important to note that this acceptance of difference may be more
difficult than it seems: "cosmopolitanism is the name not of the so-
lution but of the challenge" (xv). How do we put into practice the
attitudes that will allow us to find common cause with those who may
not share our perspectives or our particular context? How do we put
aside those structures of fear that so often (and so easily) preclude
engagement? When we find these moments of disgust, discomfort,
disindentification, can we nevertheless resist the impulse to isolate ourselves from that discomfort? Appiah suggests that perhaps we may be
more naturally cosmopolitan than we know: "Cultural purity is an
oxymoron. The odds are that, culturally speaking, you already live
a cosmopolitan life, enriched by literature, art, and film that come
from many places, and that contains influences from many more"
(*Cosmopolitanism* 113). Intellectually, we may agree with Appiah's assessment about our cosmopolitan lives, but we need only to glance
at the news to see how readily people rally around ideas (however
chimerical) of cultural purity and authenticity, with the belief that
this ostensible purity confers some sort of cultural power and authority. An essential aspect of cosmopolitan practice—and one that rarely
emerges in fundamentalist rhetoric—is the acceptance of fallibilism,
the willingness to see knowledge as something that evolves over time
and through encounters with ideas and attitudes different than one's
own. Fallibilism requires us to step back from our certainties and be
open to alternatives.

I do not mean to suggest that YA fiction offers some kind of cure
for fundamentalist certainties or that there aren't reactionary YA novels that bolster fear of the Other, but I do think that we want to
keep in mind that YA is for a readership of potential citizens—people
who have not yet, we hope, calcified into rigidity. In art—reading,
film, music, maybe even TikTok memes, if my children are to be
believed—we can encounter things that nudge us toward new structures of feeling. The phrase comes from Raymond Williams, who
references it in several different texts, perhaps most notably in *Marxism
and Literature* (1977). In its most general terms, the phrase refers to the

ways that lived experiences may vary from society's conventional narratives and expectations; that is to say, often our feelings change well before social norms and laws. And it is often in response to encounters with art that these changes begin. In *Preface to a Film*, Williams writes:

> [T]he new generation responds in its own ways to the unique world it is inheriting, taking up many continuities, that can be traced, and reproducing many aspects of the organization, which can be separately described, yet feeling its whole life in certain ways differently, and shaping its creative response into a new structure of feeling.
>
> (49)

YA fiction, I suggest, often provides the occasion for the sorts of encounters that can produce changes in structures of feeling.

YA readerships exist on the margins of their communities, and YA fiction, in turn, can demonstrate ways in which agency, community, and progressive movement can be found along the liminal edges of society. The concept of cultural purity, against which Appiah approvingly positions "contamination," fuels the fervent drawing of boundaries that position some form of "us" against some form of "other." These boundaries exist in the belief that in homogeneity there is strength. What is illustrated in the novels that I am discussing is that communities are in fact stronger if they choose to affiliate with others, to establish common cause, despite (or perhaps because of) difference. An affiliative community can form a stronger bond than a community that is presumed to exist due to some accident of birth or location. David Hollinger uses the term "affiliation" in his discussion of solidarity, which he defines as "an experience of willed affiliation" (24). "How much," he asks, "do we owe 'to our own kind'—whatever that may mean—and how much to 'strangers,' the rest of humankind?" (23).[3] The YA fiction that I discuss in this book offers responses to this question—and extends the question of obligation beyond the human to the nonhuman and the planet itself.

The work of this project could be seen, in fact, as a way to talk about YA literature that brings it into the center of a conversation not only about the cosmopolitan power of reading, but also about reading with, as Rita Felski puts it, "hopes for a less cynical and disenchanted future" (*Hooked* viii). Both YA and cosmopolitanism exist in many different iterations, from the realist drama in books like John Green's *Turtles All the Way Down* (2017) to Gene Yuen Lang's two-volume graphic novel about the Boxer Rebellion, *Boxers and Saints* (2013), to Jacqueline Woodson's ode to friendship and Tupac Shakur, *After Tupac and D Foster* (2008). Cosmopolitanism as a concept goes back to the Stoics, but more recently has encompassed not only Appiah's well-known commentary, but also concepts of cosmofeminism, as defined by Carol Breckenridge et al. in their book *Cosmopolitanism* (2002); Ursula Heise's eco-cosmopolitanism, proposed in *Sense of Place and Sense of Planet* (2008); and Rosi Braidotti's conceptions of nomadism, conceptualized in any number of essays, but collected in *Nomadic Theory* (2011). To bring YA and cosmopolitanism together thus almost seems like those old choose-your-own-adventure stories, in which different results could be created by flipping to different pages in the book. Instead of asking readers to flip back and forth between chapters, what I have done instead is assemble a selection of speculative YA novels—a category in which I include the *Harry Potter* series—in order to discuss how this fiction addresses some of the pressing issues of the past quarter-century: xenophobia, racism, nationalism, and the climate crisis. I operate from the assumption that *all* fiction, if read well, asks us to contemplate our lives and the structures of feeling that we use to organize those lives.

I am using speculative YA fiction for my case studies because, as Sarah K. Cantrell writes, speculative fiction "makes us more attuned to the world . . . [w]e are invited to imagine new worlds in order to better take care of this one" (235). While it may seem counterintuitive, the dystopian landscapes of these novels actually provide landscapes of (mild) optimism, if we are willing to realign our modes of engagement with our communities and with the planet. The radical explorations envisioned in these novels may in fact reach a wider audience precisely because they are both "YA" and "speculative," and may perhaps be read by those who might otherwise be resistant to cosmopolitan practices. Maria Tatar, in *Heroine with 1001 Faces* (2021), suggests that authors of books for young audiences "tap into a rich vein of boldness and defiance, willing to accept the label of YA author [in order to] take on ambitious projects" (266). She cites Philip Pullman's comment that "some themes, some subjects, [are] too large for adult fiction;' they can

only be dealt with adequately in a children's book" (qtd. in Tatar 266).
Speculative YA fiction, in all its manifestations, becomes an important facet of how Philip Davis, in the remit for this 'Literary Agenda' series, describes the power of the literary more generally: It "makes available much of human life that would not otherwise be existent to thought or recognizable as knowledge." As the editors of *The Rhetorical Power of Children's Literature* point out, "adolescent literature makes significant contributions to the world of ideas in ways that are similar to philosophical treatises and other forms of scholarly literature" (132). One of the most significant contributions made by the novels I discuss here has to do with how they reimagine human relationships to the planet, thus offering commentary (and perhaps even a modicum of hope) about environmental disaster. These books ask us to imagine our species as nodes on a network rather than rulers at the top of a resource pyramid.

These speculative novels can be seen as exemplary texts within the larger category of YA literature, not only because they deal with young people on the margins of their societies (or what's left of their societies), but also because of their engagement with the climate crisis. In the opening pages of *The Great Derangement* (2016), Amitav Ghosh writes,

> [I]f the urgency of a subject were indeed a criterion of its seriousness, then, considering what climate change actually portends for the future of the earth, it should surely follow that this would be the principal preoccupation of writers the world over—and this, I think, is very far from being the case.
>
> (np)

Ghosh looks for evidence of this principal preoccupation in places like *The New York Times Book Review*, the *London Review of Books*, and so forth, but discovers that when climate change comes up as a subject, it is in the context of nonfiction:

> [N]ovels and short stories are very rarely to be glimpsed within this horizon. Indeed, it could even be said that fiction that deals with climate change is almost by definition not of the kind that is taken seriously by serious literary journals: the mere mention of the subject is often enough to relegate a novel or a short story to the genre of science fiction. It is as though in

the literary imagination climate change were somehow akin to
extraterrestrials or interplanetary travel.

(7)

His point is precisely what I am highlighting here: YA speculative fiction offers us the occasion to engage with one of the essential problems
of our moment, and yet because the category of "YA" is so often relegated to the margins, the cultural work being done by these novels
gets overlooked.

The novels I consider here, like much of YA fiction in general, bring
philosophical theorizing about contemporary culture and its problems
into the mainstream of public discourse, into non-academic realms for
non-academic readers. These books offer dazzling literary skill, but
not, as Philip Pullman says, for the sake of "artistic posturing." In these
stories, engagement matters more than exclusivity or singularity, and
as a result, alternative narratives emerge that challenge conventional
dominant hierarchies. These novels answer Donna Haraway's call in
"Anthropocene, Capitalocene, Plantationocene, Chthulucene: Making Kin" (although, of course, Haraway does not mention children's
or YA literature): "we need stories big enough to gather up complexities and keep the edges open and greedy for surprising new and old
connections" (160). The speculative fictions I talk about here gather
up the complexities of contemporary culture in order to point us toward what are sometimes surprising new connections—connections
that often involve letting go of old boundaries, old attachments, old
monsters.

By bringing together cosmopolitanisms and YA speculative fiction,
I am hoping to illustrate how fiction helps us to think through the complexities of cosmopolitan practices, in both our reading and our lived
experience. These practices include the importance of conversation
rather than combat; the need to consider not only human relationships but also relationships with the nonhuman and the planet; and
the examination of our own local contexts in terms of how they might
constrain or preclude engagement with others. My thinking is in-
flected by Carol Breckenridge's comment about the importance of
feminist theory to cosmopolitanism: "feminism has learned to wres-
tle with problems and attendant possibilities while struggling to keep
the situated rather than the universal subject in the foreground" (7).

All the writers I consider here are women, and their writing highlights the fact that local contexts are not always a source of power or safety. Breckenridge et al. coin the term "cosmofeminism" as a way to generate pressure on our "understanding of cosmopolitan solidarities and networks" (9). Gender, sexuality, and climate shape our understanding of the local and the global, the past and the future; the novels that I discuss here can help us reckon with these relationships, particularly in terms of helping to shift our understandings in order to keep pace with the powerful changes happening in (and to) the world.

One of the reasons that I value YA literature is that it offers us visions of engagement that demonstrate the capacity for community building and reinvention: they are cautiously optimistic even in the face of unraveling (or unraveled) social structures. Their mixture of speculation and magic creates worlds that, while dystopian, are also enchanting. As Felski reminds us, "enchantment is a state of engagement, one in which affirmation of wonder is potentially enlivening, energizing, even ethical, encouraging a stance of openness and generosity to the world" (Felski qtd. in Rylance 173–174). In his book *Literature and the Public Good* (2016), Rick Rylance highlights a report in *The Lancet* that examines a United Nations study in which "meaningless" was the single most common word used to describe the condition of the modern world. The medical journal found this research deeply troubling: the condition of anomie (as *The Lancet* terms it) "threatens confidence in the resilience of communities, cultures, societies, and individuals. Finding meaning amongst demoralization and anomie is a live problem" (167). This study was published in 2014, and one can only imagine how much bleaker responses would look now, three years into the Covid-19 pandemic. According to a 2020 study from Mental Health America, there was an increase of more than 126,000 episodes of major depression in teenagers from 2020 to 2021—and these are only instances that got diagnosed. Other studies have shown that the shut-down of schools during the pandemic may well have worsened the situation for many young people, particularly those for whom schools offered resources that their families did not. Without making light of mental health problems or diminishing the utility of therapy and medication, enchantment and a sense of wonder may help to alleviate a sense of meaninglessness and anomie. Literature can help us, as Falconer says, "to work out new ways of living in the present" (189). The case studies presented here offer ways of engaging with society with less fear of Otherness, less emphasis on "authenticity" or "purity," less insistence on biological connections or national identities.

The thesis of this book is simple: YA literature gives us ways to think about some of the most pressing problems of the twenty-first century by offering imaginative reconceptualizations of relationships, from what it means to be a family to the ways in which humans relate to the earth itself. Elisabeth Gruner, in her study of reading in YA literature, points out that "books for teens depict teen readers as doers and suggest that their ability to read deeply, critically, and communally is crucial to the development of adolescent agency" (2). And while teenagers may exist on the margins of their communities, their books are big business: according to the Association of American Publishers, children's and YA fiction accounted for 3.72 billion dollars in 2018 publishing revenue; speculative fiction accounted for the largest share of those sales. As might be expected, pandemic-induced home-schooling and/or lockdown led to significant gains in book sales—in May 2021, the book industry reported that the "young-adult fiction category has grown by 68% year-to-date through April 2021, compared to the previous year" (Price np), in part due to TikTok: "BookTok," in which teenagers (and some not-teens) post commentary, responses, and music about books they're reading, has had a significant impact on the publishing industry, rather remarkable for something that started, as one BookTokker says, during "quarantine boredom" (Eccleshare np). BookTok has been so powerful that publishers have taken notice, partnering with influential Tokkers and creating their own BookTok sites. Given the reach of YA fiction, and the fact that its primary audience are those who are going to inherit whatever is left of the planet, we might want to think about the power of the books being made available to them.

The books that I discuss here offer "arenas of thought" that give us the space to think about seemingly disparate ideas, like definitions of citizenship and climate change. We see the impact that concepts of citizenship have on climate change and environmental destruction: if this group or that group isn't a citizen, or is somehow "other" to "us," then it's easier to plunder the resources where that group lives, destroy their ecosystems, render their landscapes unfit for habitation. And although Ghosh points out that the literature of climate change seems not to be taken seriously, environmental humanist Stephanie LeMenager reminds us that popular fiction can "inject certain topics and possibilities into daily conversation so that they are not seen as the province of elites and other supposedly marginal groups" (qtd. in Ramuglia 156). In other words, the cultural work done by YA fiction needs to be seen as a powerful tool that shapes readers' perceptions, making them receptive to—and invested in—the possibility of positive social change.

The discussions in this book are aimed at showing how YA literature offers interventions in the pressing crises that emerge from climate catastrophe and from the rise of xenophobia and nationalism. We see how cosmopolitan engagement can help establish connections across species, as in Rebecca Roanhorse's *Storm of Locusts* (2019) and Nancy Farmer's *The House of the Scorpion* (2002), or across nationality, as in *Akata Witch* (2011). This mode of engagement also requires resistance to the allure of fundamentalist narratives and binary thinking: all of the novels I discuss here are about the power of texts and about the necessity of becoming good readers who can see the world with compassion and flexibility, rather than dogmatism and fear.

One of the most concrete aspects of this positive change gets illustrated through rehabilitation of the figure of the monster: not, that is, by transforming the monster into a human, à la "Beauty and the Beast"; and not by portraying it, à la *Twilight*, as a glittering, irresistible vampire. The monsters here—jinn, clones, demons—are rehabilitated through affiliation: each is invited into a community, and becomes in fact a nexus of community. They are not transformed into anything other than themselves. Donna Haraway's comment that monsters mark the edge of community remains true: we need only look at discussions about refugees the world over to see how the discourse works: here, in "our" place, "they" usurp resources/spread disease/cause violence, and so forth. "They" are not citizens and in many instances will never be accorded citizenship; the fact that their refugee status may have been caused by wealthier countries that resist responsibility is irrelevant. "Our" community remains intact, unsullied by "them."

The line that supposedly divides them from us is the line of the monstrous, the line of something or someone that is so profoundly other that we cannot possibly bring "them" into our community for fear of contamination. The monster raises the question of purity and authenticity: what does it mean to belong and how do we define that belonging? Purity and/or belonging as defined through bloodlines cease to have any real currency in these novels: purity becomes, in fact, a destructive objective, as we have seen in *Harry Potter*, with the supremacist Death Eaters' insistence that "mudbloods" (a derogatory term for non-magical beings) be exterminated. None of the central characters that I discuss in this book are "pure": they are mixed (human) race; or mixed (nonhuman) race; or biologically nonhuman or biological anomalies. And to a greater or lesser degree, they are all considered monsters by the societies in which they live. They hover, initially, at the periphery of their communities, but over time they find new communities, formed by affiliation rather than biology or nation. In addition to fostering responsibilities toward one another, these emerging kinship groups also forge new relationships to the planet (new ways, that is, that in many respects harken back to more ancient behaviors).[4] There is allegiance to the planet rather than nation or tribe or individual self.[5]

Because cosmopolitanism is opposed to "purity," it becomes a way to ward off discourse about monstrosity, which is so often characterized as that which is impure, unclean. Purity, as we see demonstrated in these novels again and again, is a dangerous ideal, one that often leads to violence; these novels affirm the power of impurity. Cosmopolitanism is a pretty lo-fi behavior: it's conversation, talking, listening, asking questions. It's admitting mistakes and doubt; it's thinking about the stories we tell and the stories we know and the stories whose roots we need to question. Storytelling, like reading, runs through all these novels: in Nnedi Okorafor's "Nsibidi Scripts" trilogy, we meet a giant story-eating spider; Nalo Hopkinson's *Brown Girl in the Ring*, set in a post-apocalyptic Toronto, features stories and legends from Caribbean culture; stories from Navajo culture populate Rebecca Roanhorse's "Sixth World" series; Lauren Olamina, the heroine of Octavia E. Butler's *Parable* books, explains her new religion to us in parables and poems. These are all books that are about the power of texts: reading fosters community.[6] Learning to entertain multiple possibilities and stand at a remove from one's own narrative becomes key: the lesson of ironic distance, which is itself a component of cosmopolitan practice. The stories embedded in these YA novels—religious stories, folklore, fairy tales, history books, novels—show us how the worlds in the novels are being shaped, while at the same time, what we are reading can help us to shape our own worlds. In *The Deathly Hallows*, Hermione is bequeathed *Tales of Beedle the Bard* by Dumbledore, and it is with these "old kids' stories" (Rowling, *Deathly Hallows* 135) that she, Harry, and Ron begin to crack the puzzle that will enable them to defeat Voldemort. That's why "kids' books" matter—why YA literature and children's literature should be taught in universities and why the public sphere should pay attention to these genres beyond just the latest fad: it's in these books that we find strategies that might help us resist the forces that are arrayed against the health of our societies and our planet.

Organization

In part because these books are about the power of narrative and interpretation, almost every chapter focuses on a series of close readings that highlight how the text engages with contemporary issues. The close readings will also serve to familiarize readers with these texts, which I imagine will be unfamiliar to most readers of this book. The only chapter that does not offer an extensive close reading is the chapter about the *Harry Potter* series, because I am focused in that chapter on how the series as a whole serves as an example of a global text—and as a site of local knowledge and comfort for readers around the world. All the books I discuss here engage with ideas about cosmopolitan reading, monstrosity, and the relationship between local and global, ideas that, as we will see, also create crucial interventions in thinking about the threat of climate crisis.

Chapter One, "Children of the Book," examines the ways in which all these novels, including the *Harry Potter* series, emphasize the importance of texts—as if the books themselves want to remind us about the importance of books. The books that I focus on in this chapter, G. Willow Wilson's *Alif the Unseen* (2012) and Octavia Butler's *Parable of the Sower* (1993) and *Parable of the Talents* (1998), highlight the importance of becoming a good reader, which involves not only learning to be self-reflective but also being willing to entertain multiple interpretations. These YA novels remind us of the danger of "the single story," as Chimamanda Adichie calls it, and establish the importance of finding an ironic distance from oneself. Irony here is not the shrugging "whatever" sense that is so typical of adolescence but, rather, the perspective described by Bryan Turner as a prerequisite for cosmopolitan citizenship: "intellectual distance from one's own national or local culture" (57). Cosmopolitan reading demands an ironic distance; it is, as Haraway says, "about humour and serious play. It is also a rhetorical strategy and a political method" (1991, "Science, Technology" 149). What we see dramatized in Wilson's and Butler's novels is how this ironic distancing enables a commitment to others, to the larger community, and to the planet.

The second chapter, "Loving the Monsters," focuses primarily on two sets of novels, Nancy Farmer's *The House of the Scorpion* (2002) and *The Lord of Opium* (2013), and Rebecca Roanhorse's *Trail of Lightning* (2018) and *Storm of Locusts* (2019). Both duologies take place in what had been the Southwestern United States, although the landscapes have been profoundly altered by climate catastrophes—soil polluted to the point of toxicity in the Farmer novels; an epic flood that washed away most of the Western United States, in the Roanhorse books. These devastated landscapes illustrate the consequences of yoking capitalism to the rhetoric of cultural purity. Drawing on insights from Braidotti and Haraway, this chapter examines how Farmer and Roanhorse challenge conventional ideas of the human by decoupling "monstrosity" from "threat," and how that decoupling thus enables stronger and more resilient communities.

Chapter Three, "Making Bridges," explores how Nalo Hopkinson's *Brown Girl in the Ring* and Nnedi Okorafor's "Nsibidi Scripts" trilogy (2011–2022) reimagine the repressive or regressive elements of their local cultures. These novels dramatize the relationship between ancient practices and contemporary resistance that Raymond Williams articulates in his now-classic book *Marxism and Literature* (1977). In his arguments about residual, emergent, and dominant cultures, Williams observes that emergent culture "depends crucially on finding new forms or adaptions of form" (126). The novels of Hopkinson and Okorafor bring ancient spiritual practices into new contexts, challenging dominant cultures based on patriarchy and imperialism. This recontextualization calls into question the meaning and utility of "national identity," particularly in the face of climate disasters that do not recognize national borders. These novels ask us to consider if we are moving toward a "post-nation" moment and remind us that it is possible—perhaps even preferable—to operate outside of "the national."

Chapter Four, "Reading *Harry Potter* in Abu Dhabi," examines the boy wizard in the context of my teaching at NYU Abu Dhabi, where students come from almost every country in the world. Their responses to the series and, most recently, to J. K. Rowling's comments about trans people, illustrate the power of a cosmopolitan reading practice. The *Potter* books also provide a useful case study in thinking about how we define "world literature" and what gets to count as a "global text." Can a shared reading experience become, in effect, the local context from which readers extend their understanding of the world around them?

All these novels offer us the opportunity to consider how we form communities through their depictions of groups that cohere across differences that convention might deem insurmountable: how can we form bonds with the cyborg, the monsterslayer, the witch, the prophet? The communities that form around these monstrous others do so by choice rather than by any assumptions about biology, nation, or ethnicity. The affiliative communities that have taken root by the conclusions of these novels enable multiple stories rather than a single monomyth. What we see dramatized are the ways in which differences become a source of strength that enables people to realign their relationships to the world. These groups imagine themselves as nodes in a network rather than as rulers at the pinnacle of a resource pyramid. It is in this horizontal, even rhizomatic shape that these monstrous affiliations demonstrate how we might possibly forestall further climate destruction: we need to realign our relationships to one another and to the world around us.

YA fiction gives readers the opportunity to reimagine their perceptions at every level—self, nation, planet. For those readers who are themselves young adults and thus are barred by reason of age from full participation in their societies, this literature may well contribute to the shaping of their attitudes and behaviors as they come into their majority. The texts that I discuss here offer pleasures to readers of all types—the scholar who sees the interplay between Nancy Farmer's *House of the Scorpion* and Gloria Anzaldúa's *Borderlands/La Frontera* and the teenager who appreciates the Mad-Max-inflected car chases in

Roanhorse's *Trail of Lightning*. YA operates on multiple levels, which further necessitates its inclusion in discussions about the meaning and value of literary reading.

I'm writing these pages in the third year of the Covid-19 pandemic, as variants of the virus creep into countries that thought they'd weathered the worst of it, as vaccine-deniers in the United States and elsewhere fill hospital beds, while poor countries go begging for vaccines that wealthier countries are using to deliver boosters to an already vaccinated population. What are teenagers and young adults to make of this world, teetering ever closer to the brink of causing its own extinction? How can adults *not* pay attention to what they're reading—to the books that are being written for them?

Notes

1. Following in the wake of *The Outsiders* are books like *Go Ask Alice* (1971), which was presented as an anonymously autobiographical account of a girl getting "hooked on drugs"; Paul Zindel's various stories about misfits and adolescent unhappiness, such as *The Pigman* (1968) and *My Darling, My Hamburger* (1969), in which an illegal abortion changes the lives of several high school students; and Robert Cormier's *The Chocolate War* (1974). The realism in these books was often seen by adults as the cause of adolescent unrest rather than a diagnosis.
2. Fiona McCulloch's book *Contemporary British Children's Fiction and Cosmopolitanism* (2016) is one of the few studies of children's literature that draws on cosmopolitan theory for its insights. Written during the turmoil of Brexit, McCulloch's book looks at a variety of texts, primarily by Scottish writers, in order to consider what YA fiction might offer its readers—future citizens—in terms of models of empathetic world citizenship.
3. An earlier iteration of this idea appears in my article, "Witches, Monsters, and Questions of Nation: Humans and Non-Humans in *Akata Witch* and *Trail of Lightning*," published in *International Journal of Young Adult Literature* 1:1 (2020).
4. I'm using the term "kinship group" the way that Donna Haraway does in her essay "Making Kin." A fuller discussion of Haraway's ideas occurs in Chapter Two.
5. Even a casual survey of YA fiction over the past several decades would seem to suggest that these kinship groups are in fact a hallmark of YA fiction in general. Affiliative communities function as an alternative to conventional hierarchical structures and to natal kinship groups: we can think about the group of queer friends in Francesca Lia Block's *Weetzie Bat* (1989); the vampire/human/werewolf kinship group that develops over the course of the "Twilight" series; the community of friends and lovers in Scott Westerfeld's "Uglies" trilogy (2005–2007).
6. In *Cosmopolitanism*, Appiah writes: "Folktales, drama, opera, novels, short stories; biographies, histories, ethnographies; fiction or nonfiction; painting, music, sculpture, and dance: every human civilization has ways to reveal to us values we had

not previously recognized or undermine our commitment to values that we had settled into. Armed with these terms, fortified with a shared language of value, we can often guide one another, in the cosmopolitan spirit, to shared responses; and when we cannot agree, the understanding that our responses are shaped by some of the same vocabulary can make it easier to agree to disagree. All this is part of the truth about human life" (30).

1

Children of the Book

Early in G. Willow Wilson's *Alif the Unseen* (2012), a cyberpunk novel set in an unnamed Emirate in the Arabian Gulf, the novel's gray-hat computer hacker hero, Alif, has a conversation with a jinn, who calls himself Vikram the Vampire. The man and the jinn talk about stories, specifically *Alf Yeom wa Yeom* (*The Thousand and One Days*), supposedly written by the jinn as the antithesis of *Alf Layla wa Layla* (*The Thousand and One Nights*). Vikram tells Alif that humans—"banu adam"—were never meant to read the jinn-written book because it has "parallel knowledge ... meanings that are hidden from [humans]" (Wilson 104, 106). Alif, who prides himself on being a sophisticated writer of computer code and an equally sophisticated consumer of texts and ideas, is puzzled by this idea: "so the stories aren't just stories, is what you're saying. They're really secret knowledge disguised as stories." Vikram, unimpressed by this insight, tells Alif that "one could say that of all stories, younger brother" (106). The secret knowledge of stories is the focus of this chapter, although it would be even more accurate to say that I'm talking about becoming a *reader* of those stories, someone who is willing to accept that the secret knowledge is there and to engage with stories—narratives of all sorts—at all levels of meaning.

Like the other books I discuss here, *Alif the Unseen* is deeply invested in the power of books and the need for good readers, whose ability to find the "knowledge disguised as stories" comes from a willingness to engage with the world openly and with the awareness, as we will see, that error and recalibration are inevitable and essential. All of these novels illustrate the links between becoming good readers and reimagining structures of citizenship and community: When we develop the ability to discern the "secret knowledge" in stories, we also develop the ability to ask questions about the stories we carry inside ourselves and the stories in which society embeds us. We see, for instance, in Octavia E. Butler's *Parable of the Sower* (1993) that Lauren Olamina's father, an intelligent man trained as a preacher, is blind to the realities of climate crisis because he insists on seeing only Biblical truth; Ti-Jeanne, in Nalo Hopkinson's *Brown Girl in the Ring* (1998), barters her grandmother's herbal remedies for books, but the more important stories are those of the "spirits ... loas ... orishas" (126), which hold the lessons she needs to save her child and her community. Sunny Nwazue, in Nnedi Okorafor's *Akata Witch*, discovers that she is part of a secret order of magical people called Leopards, whose governing council is headquartered in a magical library and convened by a woman known as the Chief Librarian. In order to avoid becoming a tyrant like his genetic progenitor, the clone at the center of Nancy Farmer's *House of Scorpion* duology must learn from the counternarratives and legends that circulate in the borderlands; and texts of all sorts appear in the "Harry Potter" series. In all of these examples, becoming a better reader fosters resistance to nationalism and xenophobia and enables a more cosmopolitan, nonhierarchical relationship to the planet.

In "Cosmopolitan Reading" (qtd. in Dharwadker 207), Appiah urges us "to see the novel as a testing ground for a distinction between cosmopolitanism, with its emphasis on dialogue among differences and a different more monological form of humanism." Elsewhere, Appiah argues that fiction provides us with the opportunity to engage in these dialogues:

> What we find in the novel, which is always a message in a bottle from some other position, even if it was written and published last week in your hometown, derives not from a theoretical understanding of us as having a commonly understood common nature—not, then, from an understanding that we (readers and writers) all share—but from an invitation to respond in imagination to narratively constructed situations.
>
> (Appiah, "Rooted Cosmopolitanism" 257)

These "messages in a bottle" bob across our consciousness, and as we take in their contents, we find worlds of possibility that may enable us to transform our own worlds, through reimagining local contexts that repress or silence difference, realigning structures of feeling, and—essential for this moment in planetary history—reimagining our relationship to the planet.

To illustrate the links between reading and cosmopolitan citizenship, this chapter will focus on Butler's two *Parable* novels and Wilson's *Alif the Unseen*, books that also exemplify the texts-within-texts aspect that is widespread in so much YA fiction. As "messages in a bottle," Butler's and Wilson's novels extend Appiah's ideas and highlight what Ursula Heise has called "eco-cosmopolitanism," which she defines in a *Sense of Place and Sense of Planet* (2008). Eco-cosmopolitanism builds on cosmopolitan theories and "reaches toward what some environmental writers and philosophers have called the 'more-than-human world'—not only the realm of nonhuman species, but also animate and inanimate networks of influence and exchange" (Heise 60–62). Heise's reformulation widens our conceptions of cosmopolitanism and connects to what we will see happening in the novels I discuss here. As these adolescent characters become better readers—of texts, of myths, of themselves—their understanding of how they fit into larger planetary and nonhuman networks also expands.

The *Parable* books and *Alif the Unseen* are "road novels" about marginalized figures whose experiences with texts enable them to reimagine and (potentially) restructure their communities. These novels also illustrate the inevitable upheavals that accompany social change and the role(s) that sacred texts might play in such changes. In stressing the importance of reading and texts, these books might be thought to be preaching to the choir: They are, after all, showing their readers the importance of reading. But they also illustrate the connection between reading and community engagement and between reading and the ability to imagine alternative ways of planetary connection, and, perhaps most importantly, the need to relinquish narratives that insist on purity or authenticity, which almost always lead to destruction. The stories that rest on simple binaries or that refuse dialogic engagement lead, all too easily, to the rise of totalitarianism and planetary collapse. These novels hold out the hope that by becoming readers willing to engage with capacious story-making, we can find modes of engagement that work against tyranny and climate crisis.

Section One: *Parables*

Early in *Parable of the Sower* (1993), set in 2024 California, seventeen-year-old Lauren Olamina compiles all the writing that she's been doing into a single notebook. The notes all have to do with a new religion that will challenge the beliefs of her preacher father and, Lauren hopes, open a path for people to find new spiritual practices. She wants all her writing in one place so that she can more easily pack it into the go-bag she's readying against what she's sure will be an attack on the gated community where she lives. This pile of notebooks will become the founding documents of Earthseed, a religion whose principles of nomadism, evolution, and multiplicity will collide with a decaying society's insistence on fundamentalist certainties. Butler never uses the world "cosmopolitanism" in these novels, but Lauren's belief in the importance of conversation, her willingness to engage with difference, and her acceptance of fallibilism suggest that in her religious and spiritual thinking, there is a cosmopolitan ethos at work.

Lauren comes to her ideas as the country around her frays and disintegrates; her father says that the United States is "barely a nation anymore" (*Sower* 15). Robledo, the gated community where she lives, is not gated because of its wealth or exclusivity but as an effort to keep out the murderous gangs that roam what used to be the suburbs of what used to be Los Angeles. The community knows that if they're attacked, they can't depend on anyone other than themselves for help; there is no longer a functioning police force, especially not for people of color.[1] Many of the gangs are hooked on a drug called pyro that makes watching fires better than sex. Water has become more expensive than fuel, and the only people who use gas-powered engines are "arsonists and the rich" (14). Against this grim backdrop, Lauren's father insists that if they stay vigilant inside the gates, they will survive; he also insists, despite years of drought, that humans couldn't have caused climate change: "only God could change the world in such an important way" (47). In 1993, many of Butler's readers may have agreed with that thought. Climate change was being discussed, but not with the urgency that we now realize was needed.[2]

Contrary to her father's dogmatism, Lauren thinks that change is both necessary and urgent. She is also sure that people need to be "pried loose from the rotting past [toward] building a future that makes sense" (68). The move from past to future hinges on embracing rather than resisting change, which is the central tenet of her new spiritual practice: "All that you touch, you change. All that you Change, Changes you. The only lasting truth is Change. God is Change" (68). Evolving will be the only way to survive what's coming, she tells her friend Joanna as they stand outside marveling at the first rain in six years, "good, clean free water from the sky" (39) that unfortunately does not last long enough to alleviate the drought. Lauren lists all the problems facing the country: In addition to pyro, the fire-addictive drug, there are tornadoes in other parts of the country, a measles epidemic, and a blizzard in the Midwest, while the newly elected President Donner plans to sell off bits of the country to the highest bidder. Joanna's response to Lauren's list of travails is that Lauren has been "reading too many adventure stories." Lauren doesn't dispute the accusation; she just encourages Joanna to find and read any books she can that might be useful: books on foraging, plants and animals, descriptions of the landscape; "even some fiction might be useful," she adds.[3]

Joanna misses the point of Lauren's suggestion and tells her that "books aren't going to save us" (49), and, in a way, Joanna is right. Books can't stop the pyros who attack Robledo and kill everyone they can find, including Joanna. Lauren manages to escape, in part because she has prepared herself for this cataclysm. In her "go-bag," along with tampons and money, are books. The books don't help her deal with the loss of her stepmother and brothers, but because she is a good reader, she knows she should head north in an effort to escape the escalating violence. With Harry and Zahra, two other survivors of the attack, Lauren starts walking, in an echo of the journey taken by people escaping from slavery in the antebellum South. Like those forebears, Lauren and her companions think that perhaps they can find refuge in Canada, if they can survive the dangerous journey. To lessen the risk, Lauren dresses herself as a man; she and Zahra will pass as an African American couple traveling with Harry, "their white friend" (172). As they prepare for their journey, scavenging whatever supplies they can find from the wreckage of Robledo, Lauren tells Zahra that it is important to gather knowledge from every source. Much to Zahra's surprise, Lauren says that she too is a teacher, despite being illiterate: "You're going to be one of my teachers ... Everyone who's surviving out here knows things that I need to know . . . . I'll watch them. I'll listen to them, I'll learn from them" (173). Zahra's experiences, in other words, will become the text that Lauren will learn to read, just as they all learn to read the old maps that they use to chart their course north.

While Lauren is certain about the necessity and inevitability of change, she also understands the importance of admitting what she doesn't know, of admitting that her frame of reference—as an educated and relatively privileged young woman—is not the only one that matters. Lauren's willingness to learn from "everyone" and her belief that everyone has something to offer suggest a cosmopolitanism practice at work: engaging across difference, being comfortable with fallibilism. *Parable of the Sower* is littered with texts, from the Bible that Lauren's preacher father uses to the "western novel" that Harry buys from a street vendor to Lauren's own writings about Earthseed. As a reader and a student, Lauren gathers ideas wherever she can, refusing to be constrained by conventional narratives.

In both *Parable of the Sower* and its sequel, *Parable of the Talents* (1998), becoming a good reader means becoming a good citizen—and key to both is learning to tolerate uncertainty while searching for a baseline of understanding. Lauren refines and alters her ideas about Earthseed through conversations, discussions, and arguments. When she talks to Travis, one of the people who joins her on the journey north, she "trie[d] to answer his questions without preaching a sermon, which was hard" (*Sower* 223). The practice of cosmopolitanism requires that we listen and consider rather than preach, that we ask questions rather than insist on orthodoxy. As the group walking north grows and as more conversations take place, Lauren begins to imagine what Earthseed could be: a community where they could "provide education plus reading and writing services . . . so many people, children and adults are illiterate these days" (224). Embedded in Lauren's ideas about building a new community in which the only certainty is change is the importance of reading and writing—an idea that Butler amplifies in the sequel, which links illiteracy with the rise of violent fundamentalism.

Parable of the Talents foregrounds the importance of reading and education by demonstrating how easily an ignorant population can be manipulated by a demagogue. When Andrew Jarret becomes president, at the beginning of this novel—having run on a campaign to

"Make America Great Again"—he is at the forefront of the Christian America (CA) movement, a fundamentalist militaristic group that sees witches everywhere: "a Moslem [sic], a Jew, a Hindu, a Buddhist, or in some parts of the country, a Mormon, a Jehovah's Witness, or even a Catholic ... [or] an atheist, a 'cultist,' or a well-to-do-eccentric ... [President] Jarret's people have been known to beat or drive out Unitarians, for goodness sake" (*Talents* 19). What makes CA members so easily led, Lauren thinks, is that more than half the country "can't read [and] history is just one more vast unknown" (19).

If *Sower* was about Lauren's search to establish Earthseed, then *Talents* is about how to enable an unconventional community and ideology to flourish, without dogmatism, orthodoxy, or tyranny. Acorn, the tiny community that has only just begun at the conclusion of *Sower*, has more than seventy inhabitants at the opening of the second book—and yet, despite its small size and remote location, it is perceived as a threat by CA. All Acorn residents are taught reading and numeracy, many speak English and Spanish, and everyone contributes to the well-being of the community. The community of racially and ethnically mixed children are raised collectively: "Family," in Acorn, does not necessarily connote biological relationship. Acorn exists on land that belongs to Taylor Franklin Bankole, who becomes Lauren's lover midway through *Sower*. For all that Acorn exists in a fixed spot—Bankole's family land—the principles that guide the community foster flux and evolution. Ironically, it is precisely because of this flexibility that Acorn must patrol its boundaries, guarding against fundamentalist vigilantes who want to eradicate anything they see as diverging from "Christian" principles. The fundamentalism of Jarret's CA movement and the cosmopolitanism of Earthseed collide when Lauren finds her long-lost brother Marcus. She thought he'd died in the attack on Robledo five years earlier, but he'd ended up enslaved to a series of pimps who kept him in an electric collar. Marcus, who now calls himself Marcos, does not understand how Earthseed works in terms of its origins or its practices. Lauren tells him that while the land belongs to Bankole, Acorn is "our place ... it doesn't belong to me" (*Talents* 125). The community works as a collective, she explains, and while she has the title of "Shaper," she is not the boss or the leader in any conventional sense of the word.

Somewhat surprisingly for a man who has been enslaved, Marcos believes that hierarchies are essential because they preserve order; Earthseed's principles seem to him chaotic and impractical. He doesn't understand the synthesis of ideas that led to Earthseed, despite Lauren's explanation: "[A]ll the truths of Earthseed existed somewhere else before I found them and put them together. They were in the patterns of history, in science, philosophy, religion, or literature. I didn't make any of them up" (126). By reading widely, Lauren makes connections, creating a flexible set of paradigms that evolve and shift as needed. Marcos rejects this nonhierarchical thinking and attempts to preach to the community, with disastrous results. He insists that God doesn't change and is enraged when Zahra tells him that "our God isn't male. Change has no sex. Marc, you don't know enough about us yet even to criticize us" (151). Her comment is accurate. Marcos cannot or will not admit what he doesn't know, an attitude that even extends into the ways he participates in the work of the community: He makes mistakes because "it bothered him that he had so much to learn" (151). An Acornite yells at him after he almost damages one of their hard-to-find farm tools: "[I]f you don't know, *ask* . . . Nobody expects you to know everything. Just ask" (151). Lauren and the other Acorn residents—even those who have, like Marcos, escaped from slavery—are willing to accept doubt and uncertainty, an ongoing reminder about the importance of fallibilism in the process of learning about the world.

The Acorn community, true to the principles of Earthseed, operates in the messy space of conversations that give everyone an equal voice, an equal right to speak. Lauren tells Marcos that all of Acorn's community meetings, called Gatherings, involve "questions, challenges, argument . . . we learn as much by discussion as by lecture, demonstration, or experience" (157). This process can be chaotic, disorderly, and slow; it means engaging with points of view that might be different from one's own in order to learn. Marcos cannot accept what to him seems like such a radical structure, and he leaves Acorn to join (as we discover later) Jarret's CA as a preacher and missionary. Six months after his departure, the CA storms Acorn and renames it "Camp Christian." Its members enslave Lauren and others, kill those who try to resist, and send all the children, including Lauren and Bankole's daughter Larkin, to "good Christian homes."

During their eighteen months of enslavement, the Acorn members are "re-educated" through torture and forced memorization of Bible verses; the CA jailers destroy the classroom spaces, burn the books, and keep their captives in electronic choke collars.

After a rare and fortuitous thunderstorm knocks out the power on the choke collars, enabling a mass escape, Lauren and her community begin the slow process of rebuilding Earthseed, using whatever tools they can to enable conversations. Joel Elford, one of the new members of the community, tells her that her book about Earthseed should be "free on the nets" (*Talents* 390), a sign of optimism that now seems antiquated—although Lauren's hesitation seems prescient: She worries that the book will become "an instrument of some other theology or . . . brand-new demagoguery." Joel tells her not to fear, because he has "aimed the book at the nets that are intended to interest American universities and the smaller free cities where so many of those universities are located" (390). This belief in the egalitarian nature of the internet may seem incredibly naïve to those of us living in the age of the algorithm, but we might remember that in the earliest days of personal computing, the internet was going to bring worlds and communities together by creating frictionless engagement and accountability. Lauren decides that the need for more connections outweighs the risks, and Earthseed expands toward what she calls its "starry Destiny." As if in anticipation of Ursula Heise's ideas about eco-cosmopolitanism, Lauren believes that Earthseed can be a "long-term success and the parents . . . of a vast array of new peoples, new species . . . [if] we . . . scatter the Earth's living essence—human, plant, and animal—to extrasolar worlds" (45). The propulsion of Earthseed away from earth is facilitated by the training of its children, who are urged to go to university and "pursue any course of study." There is no dogma in Earthseed, only a drive to find, as Heise describes it, a sense of "connectedness with both animate and inanimate networks of influence and exchange" (Heise 60).

Surprisingly, the person most critical of the "starry Destiny" is Lauren's daughter Larkin, who was kidnapped when CA captured Acorn and sent to live with a CA family. This family taught her to "believe *absolutely* in God, in Jarret, and in being good Christian Americans . . . quiet was good. Questioning was bad" (*Talents* 264). As a result of her upbringing, Larkin never questions the CA narrative, even though her own experience contradicts the idea that she was raised by "good Christians." Her foster father tries repeatedly to rape her and her foster mother thinks the attacks are Larkin's fault. And yet, even after Larkin earns a PhD in history, she clings to her certainty. She may be educated, but she refuses to ask any questions that might disturb the narrative with which she's grown up. She should be a better reader than she is, and one of her significant failings is the inability to recognize her own shortcomings.

Larkin's adherence to the official story seems all the more curious when we discover that in addition to being a historian, she writes popular virtual-reality programs. Under the name Asha Vere (the name her foster parents gave to her and also the name of a popular character in the Dreamasks), she writes scripts for Dreamasks, computer simulation stories that enable people to "live their character's fiction life . . . submerge themselves in other, simpler, happier lives" (219). Larkin invents these scenarios, but the dreams inside the masks change nothing: The people who buy the scripted stories are passive consumers rather than engaged partners. Even though she writes dreams for a living, Larkin refuses to appreciate Lauren's dream of moving Earthseed to space. In fact, it's Lauren's fixation on "starry Destiny" that Larkin hates most about her mother. Larkin wants something much more earthbound and traditional, something more local and domestic: She thinks Lauren should focus solely on cleaning up the "various hells we've made right here on earth" (377).

In her desire for Lauren to stay local, as it were—for Acorn to be only a "refuge for the homeless and the orphaned"—Larkin occupies the position of those in Plato's cave allegory who resent being told that they are looking at shadows, not reality. Neither Larkin nor the inhabitants of the cave want to hear about what might be possible if they look outside the cave, if they listen to another set of narratives. Larkin values her uncle Marc, who "wanted to make Earth a better place. Uncle Marc knew that the stars could take care of themselves." Larkin can't hear the implicit hierarchy in "take care," which positions one entity as being obligated to another. Earthseed is about partnership: "giving, taking, learning, teaching . . . Partner diverse communities. Partner any world that is your home . . . Only in partnership can we thrive, grow, Change" (136). Thinking in terms of partnerships rather than power threatens structures of power.

Lauren lives long enough to see Earthseed's destiny fulfilled, although even in the moment of fulfillment, there is a warning. The spaceships are full of "people and animals and seeds and books," but they are headed to a space station that's been named Christopher Columbus, a name that undercuts the idea of scattering the earth's essence. Lauren tries unsuccessfully to get the name of the space station changed because the Earthseed mission is not "a shortcut to riches and empires . . . snatching up slaves and gold" (394). The name of the space station warns us about the failures of human nature: Can we go forward (or outward) without replicating the destructive impulses of colonialism and capitalism?

The conclusion of *Talents* shows us that change will not occur without loss, but it also demonstrates a possible answer to Braidotti's question about "how [we] turn mourning and loss of the natural order into effective action" (*Nomadic Theory* 352). That transformation, Braidotti says, will require a "multiplicity of possible cartographies"—such as, let's imagine, extrasolar communities—where, let's imagine, different species can meet, perhaps breed, create post-human entities and communities. The end of *Parable of the Talents* literally moves humans away from their center of gravity into new orbits: The polyglot, mixed-race, multigenerational, affiliated community floats into space, where its first action will be resisting the premise of exploration embedded in the name Christopher Columbus. We are given, in Braidotti's terms, a vision of "renewed conceptual creativity and a leap of the social imaginary" (355), but in order to make these leaps, we need to learn how to read beyond conventional narratives, reinterpret orthodoxies, and become comfortable with multiplicities that might be chaotic and inefficient.

Section Two: *Alif the Unseen*

Also a road novel concerned with sacred texts, G. Willow Wilson's *Alif the Unseen* offers a more cynical view of "the nets" than does *Parable of the Talents*, as befits a narrative set in the early twenty-first century with a protagonist who writes code for a living. Alif (we never learn his last name) lives in an unnamed Emirate in the Arabian Gulf, in The City, which seems like a combination of Cairo and Dubai. When Alif comes into possession of something called the *Alf Yeom wa Yeom*

(*The Thousand and One Days*), a collection of jinn-written tales that are the inverse of *Alf Layla wa Layla* (*The Thousand and One Nights*), he unwittingly becomes the target of the authoritarian State, represented by a man known as The Hand, who designs cyber-security for The City and who is, unknown to Alif, the fiancé of Intisar, the princess with whom Alif has had a short-lived affair. The Hand despises Alif for "sullying" his bride-to-be, but he also hates Alif for writing code that enables people to elude The Hand's digital police. Alif calls himself a gray-hat hacker, a polite way of saying that he's a mercenary who will write code for anyone who pays him. The programs he writes enable websites for porn, chat rooms, gaming, and gambling to operate in countries where such things are against the law. The only thing Alif actively resists, he tells his next-door neighbor Dina, are censors, and to that end, he will "help anybody with a computer and a grudge" (231).

At the beginning of the novel, Alif is whiny and self-involved, sure that he is the center of attention and yet eternally the victim. He is certain, for example, that Intisar broke up with him because he's not pure Arab: His Indian mother is the second wife of his Arab father, who has nothing to do with his second family. Alif thinks he's handsome enough, but "nothing less than full-blood, inherited from a millennium of sheikhs and emirs, was enough for Intisar" (12). He is dismissive of his friend Dina because she wears hijab, but he sees Intisar's veil as a sign of mystery and elegance. When Dina returns Alif's copy of *The Golden Compass*, Philip Pullman's fantasy about an alternative universe wherein England is a theocracy and everyone has an externalized soul called a daemon, she says the book is "full of pagan images. It's dangerous."[4] Alif disregards her comment, saying that her English isn't good enough to understand Pullman's use of metaphor, but Dina persists: "[M]etaphors are dangerous . . . calling something by a false name changes it, and metaphor is just a fancy way of calling something by a false name" (11). Wilson's novel interrogates this claim: *Are* metaphors dangerous? Are Pullman's metaphors as dangerous as government malfeasance hiding behind an innocuous cloak of neutral-seeming nouns? Is it dangerous to reframe culpability to avoid responsibility, which Braidotti notes often happens in discussions of climate change: "[T]he dominant discourse has become . . . utterly irresponsible in perpetuating anthropocentric arrogance and denial of the man-made structure of catastrophe [which] we continue to attribute to forces beyond our collective control—the earth, the cosmos, or 'nature'" (352). After all, if something is natural, we cannot possibly hope to change it, can we? Dina's comment resonates through the novel, asking us (and Alif) to consider how metaphors work and how we can learn to hold multiple meanings in our minds simultaneously.

Alif has no interest in climate crisis or almost anything else, other than his passion for Intisar and hatred for digital censors. He barely registers the women around him: When his mother annoys him with her requests that he find a bride among his own kind, he flings a plate of food on the ground and then steps over the maid who is cleaning up his mess. The novel portrays the layered realities of life in the Gulf, from the elite ruling class to the myriad guest workers who exist at every point on the economic ladder, from university professors to the "chaiwallah" who operates a snack kiosk at the tourist attractions. Alif is, like so many other YA protagonists, an unlikely hero. But unlike other ordinary-turned-extraordinary characters, such as Harry Potter, Pullman's Lyra Belacqua, or Luke Skywalker in *Star Wars*, Alif is not motivated by any higher purpose other than saving his own skin and protecting Dina, who inadvertently gets tangled in Alif's mess. Alif believes in no cause, doesn't see himself pursuing some righteous mission. The novel's thick intertextual references to stories about righteous heroes—to the Potterverse, *Star Trek*, *World of Battlecraft*, *Star Wars*, and so on—highlight how ill-suited Alif is to the task of fighting against the powers of the State: "Righteousness" is not something that Alif spends much time thinking about.

Alif prides himself on having sophisticated literary taste, but he is not a good reader because he has no sense of wonder or engagement. Until he met Vikram, he thought stories were just stories; he was convinced that everything could be solved with lines of code and his laptop. Learning the truth of Vikram's comment is at the heart of Alif's journey, just as the power of story and the importance of becoming a good reader are at the heart of this novel, which also details the start of the Arab Spring. Alif tells Vikram that the reason it's easy to get fantasy novels in his city is that "censors don't bother with fantasy books, especially old ones. They can't understand them. They think it's all kids' stuff" (104). He is dismissive of the censors but does not consider that his own understanding of this "kids' stuff" is superficial, at best.

The novel's intertextuality centers on two actual texts, the Quran and *Alf Layla*, and one imagined—the *Alf Yeom*—whose magically shifting, jinn-authored tales mirror those in *Alf Layla*.[5] Intisar had been writing her thesis on *Alf Yeom* and she gives the book to Alif in order to keep the book away from her thuggish fiancé. When Alif hacks into Intisar's computer, he reads her thesis, which is about *Alf Yeom* and the spiritual crisis it sparks: Intisar cannot reconcile why "young degree-holding traditionalists" interpret Islamic law as "sacrosanct" but refuse to accept the existence of "djinn . . . [and] hidden people." Her document ends with "I do not know what to believe" (111). Alif doesn't believe in jinn, even after he meets Vikram, and he "failed to pick up on the clues" that Intisar was having a crisis of faith. In every context, Alif is a bad reader. He imagines himself at the center of every narrative and his world-view is limited to lines of code; he is not equipped for a world that extends beyond his empirical understanding.

At the outset of the journey that is triggered by the gift of *Alf Yeom*, Alif thinks like a computer program, and his binary operating system does not allow for anything that might seem "irrational." When Alif and Dina are chased by government minions who are searching for *Alf Yeom*, they take refuge with Alif's hacker friend Abdullah, who suggests that they need to go "off the grid" if they hope to avoid capture. He tells them to go to the old souk and look for Vikram the Vampire, which Alif finds laughable. He thinks Vikram is just a kids' story, an old legend with no basis in reality. Abdullah says otherwise: "[H]e's a black market thug" who will help them for money. Like Alif, Vikram is a mercenary. When Dina and Alif find Vikram, it is Dina who points out what Alif doesn't understand: "[Y]ou read all those *kuffar* fantasy novels and yet you deny something straight out of a holy book" (92). Through her reading of the Quran, Dina is open to the possibility of wonder, to the presence of the hidden people, while Alif, the supposed sophisticate, can only suggest that they break their experience "into its composite parts until it makes some kind of rational sense" (93). He can only imagine the strategy he uses for coding—linear, rational, empirical. His limitations highlight one of the goals that Wilson said she had for the novel: "[W]e live in this ultra-rational age where anything wonderful, magical or transcendent is somehow suspect, and

I think we've lost something important because of that. I want to bring that wonder and awe back a little bit" (*The National* np). One of the tasks confronting Alif will be a reconsideration of his insistence on binary modes of thinking that keep rational and irrational, faith and technology as opposites.

The modes of writing in Wilson's novel, from the *Alf Yeom* to the Quran to Java and C+++, spiral into one another and, if we pay attention, show us how to read across histories and societies, layering meanings instead of severing them.[6] As Alif tries to figure out why he is being chased by the government and why they want the *Alf Yeom*, he recovers his sense of wonder and, in so doing, finds a more ethical and generous way in which to engage with the world. In the introduction to her magisterial study of *The Arabian Nights*, Marina Warner addresses the importance of this sense of wonder using the word *aja'ib*—"marvels, wonders, astonishing things"—which she says has offered writers across history "a chance for exuberant play to envision, as Shahrazad herself does in the stories, different régimes of authority, emancipated erotics, and prophetic technological innovations . . . They picked up on the deep dynamic of the book: that Shahrazad through her stories is persuading the tyrannical Sultan to think again" (28). Learning to read with a sense of wonder, allowing ourselves the experience of engaging with multiple interpretations and possibilities, may lead us to "think again" about how we see our worlds and our relationships to these worlds. Warner describes the tales of *The Arabian Nights* as enacting an "endlessly generative" pattern of arabesque that stretches in all directions. The interlocking and entwined nature of the tales operates not only within the collection but beyond it: The tales "spill out from the covers of the volumes in which they appear . . . they escape from the limits of time that the narrative struggles to impose. They keep generating more tales, in various media, themselves different but alike: the stories themselves are shapeshifters" (7). *Alif the Unseen* might be characterized as one of these tales, spiraling in and out of the ancient text, while also updating it through the creation of yet another interlocking text, the *Alf Yeom, The Thousand and One Days*.

Initially, Alif uses his abilities as a reader and as a writer solely to spy on Intisar, telling himself that he's watching her only to make sure that she's okay. Without knowing precisely how he's done it, he writes a computer program that he names with the anagram Tin Sari, which can identify people through their keystrokes. Tin Sari hides Alif's identity, and Intisar doesn't know he's there, thus turning Alif into a computer daemon, lurking in the background. Stunned by his invention, Alif wonders if

> somewhere deep in the mind was a sort of linguistic DNA, rope helixes of symbols that belonged to no one else ... how much of the soul resided in the fingertips[?] He was faced with the possibility that every word he typed spoke his name, no matter what other superficial relationship it might contain. Perhaps it was impossible to become someone else, no matter what avatar or handle one hid behind.
>
> (44)

His question offers a digital-age version of eternal questions about the nature of the soul, and the relationship between writing and self. Does Tin Sari strip away the metaphor of language to reveal some sort of essential self? Can we ever hope to reach such an essence? Metaphysics aside, Tin Sari is also a powerful stalking device, a tool that The Hand wants for his own use in order to track and punish hackers like Alif.

The Hand, like Andrew Jarret and Marcos in the *Parable* novels, wants to control the narrative in order to maintain absolute dominance and enforce orthodoxy. The Hand presents himself as a man of faith, but he uses religion as a tool to control the "disaffected scum," his term for anyone who is not a member of the royal family. Initially he hunts for Alif because he finds out about Tin Sari, but when he finds out that Alif has *Alf Yeom*, the hunt intensifies. Both The Hand and Alif recognize that the jinn stories could be used as a coding source, "translating strings of metaphors into strings of commands ... [following the writers of the book] who developed a system of transmitting knowledge that could accommodate the contradictions" (229). *Alf Yeom* shape-shifts; its contents change depending on who is reading. This fluidity will ultimately prove to be The Hand's undoing: Like most tyrants, he cannot tolerate ambiguity or multiplicity.

On the run from The Hand and his minions, Alif takes refuge in a mosque, knowing that his pursuers will think twice before following him inside; it is a pragmatic decision rather than a theological one. The mosque's imam, Sheikh Bilal, chastises Alif for not removing his shoes or cleaning up the muddy tracks he leaves on the floor, but he ultimately lets Alif hide in a back room. When he asked Alif why he was in trouble, Alif "smiled contemptuously" and tried to explain the nature of his computer program and of quantum computing more generally. He assumes, as he did with Dina, that a man of faith would not be able to understand technology. As he was with Dina, Alif is surprised by Bilal's insights, which he expresses "in language from [his] own field of study." Bilal tells him that according to ancient scholars, "each word in the Quran has seven thousand layers of meaning, each of which . . . exist equally at all times without cosmological contradiction. Is this similar to what you mean?" (192). Even as Alif is startled by Bilal's ideas, he lacks the ability to do more than offer a superficial appreciation, because he has never thought about how language or religion works. Bilal tells him that he looks like a boy "who shirks his religious education" (192); he reads Alif better than Alif reads himself.

Because Alif is so sure of himself, he makes mistakes without realizing it, and his hubris—more than once—almost gets him killed. Inspired by Bilal's comments about the Quran, he decides he can write a program that will defeat The Hand and feels "an almost erotic surge of excitement" when the Linux platform on Bilal's old computer loads up. His plan brings us back to the conversation he had with Dina about *The Golden Compass*: "Metaphors: knowledge existing in several states simultaneously and without contradiction . . . the computer could work with bundles that were one and zero and every point in between . . . if, if, if, you could teach it to overcome its binary nature" (227). Bilal thinks it's blasphemy to use the Quran as the basis for a computer program, and Alif assures him that he is going to use *Alf Yeom* instead. He chooses to ignore Vikram's warnings that no human can reckon with the jinn-authored book, which is changeable "depending on who reads it." The book is mutable, a living text, and it is this quality that Alif hopes to build into a computer program. Coding itself, in fact, might be seen as metaphoric, in that the strings of ones and zeros produce something other than themselves; they create another layer of meaning, just as metaphors do. Fundamentalist discourse—like CA, or the authoritarianism of The Hand—wants to repress metaphor.

As Alif starts to code, the beautiful Princess Farukhuaz from the stories appears to him in a vision, becoming more and more real to him as he works. She urges him to destroy the mainframe that The Hand built, and Alif writes faster and faster, losing himself in unity with the machine—until the edifice he's constructed begins to crumble: "[I]n his zeal for innovation he had sacrificed the integrity of his knowledge" (240). Farukhuaz, with her seductive voice and gold-ringed hands, has tricked him in the same way Intisar had fooled him, by letting him think he was the hero of his own narrative, the rescuer of the damsel in distress.

Lulled into complacency by a familiar (albeit false) story about being the hero, Alif thought he was being initiated into something powerful and elite, but which proved to be "pointless secrecy." His self-importance becomes something "tawdry" and he is forced to confront his own "failure of imagination" (238). As the program collapses, The Hand breaks into the mosque and is about to capture his friends. But this moment of crucial failure leads to Alif's development as a cosmopolitan reader. His program has collapsed, but he holds himself accountable instead of blaming circumstance, the machine, or other people. "I've screwed up," he says. "Dina was right—the sheikh was right—[Vikram] was right" (241). Alif's failure forces him to admit that others have knowledge that matters, that other operating systems, as it were, have power. The faith-based epistemologies of Bilal and Dina, and of Vikram, deserve respect, even if they are different from his own. The systems that deserve to be challenged and dismantled are those that attempt to control and silence others.

Reading more carefully and being more attuned to multiple interpretations and perspectives gives Alif new ways of thinking about himself and his relationship to the world. His shifting perspectives embody what Rita Felski says about reading with engagement rather than suspicion: We can "imagine ourselves as a different kind of person . . . work our way into having different values . . . care about new things" (*Hooked* 128). We might also think about the fact that Alif, when he's working with his computer, almost transcends the human, as Edward Ardeneaux points out in his essay about speculative fiction and the revolutionary imagination. Ardeneaux suggests that the hacker figure is embedded in "technologies of distributed and extended cognition . . . hacker characters inhabit posthuman subjectivities more obviously than other posthumans" (375). Lest this description seem far-fetched, we remember the "almost erotic" feeling Alif has as he boots up Linux and then the smell of "burning flesh" as the machine melts. Vikram finds Alif in the mosque by following his scent, which "reeks of electricity and hot metal," and later a demon calls Alif "chemical man," saying that he stinks of "copper wire and rare earth elements and electricity" (199, 313). Alif unifies machine and human, just as later he will learn to write code that unifies faith and tech: The boundaries blur into irrelevance.

The shape-shifting Vikram offers another lesson about what becomes possible when conventional boundaries and narratives are relinquished. Vikram appears as a king in *Alf Yeom*, is seen as a dog by Bilal and a hyena by Alif; Vikram is everything, that is, except an actual vampire (although he does occasionally hang upside down like a bat). He is also the ardent pursuer of a woman known only as The Convert, an academic who works at Basheera University, and whose advice Alif and Vikram seek about the origins of *Alf Yeom*. Despite having converted to Islam and learned Arabic, The Convert still feels that she is a foreigner: "[D]o you know how many words for foreigner I know? ... *Ajanib. Ferenghi. Khawagga. Gori. Pardesi.* And I've been called all of them. They're not nice words" (157). The insults converge like metaphors, layers of meaning with shades of nuance: *ferenghi* comes from Persian and suggests stranger or European; *gori* comes from Hindu and technically refers to "white girl"; and so on. The Convert feels the sting of marginalization, but she expresses her indignation in terms of a kind of *noblesse oblige*, as if she cannot imagine why anyone would be anything other than grateful at the fact of her conversion:

> [I]t doesn't matter to you what concessions we make ... dress respectfully, learn the language, follow all the insane rules about when to speak and how and to whom .... I even adopted your religion, adopted out of my own free will, thinking I was doing something noble and righteous ... [but] I'll always be foreign.
>
> (157)

The Convert cannot hear the self-righteousness in her tone, but she knows enough about the social hierarchy of The City to be able to manipulate the systems to her advantage. Because she is "a white American with a blue passport," she will serve as the "ultimate escort" and smuggle Alif onto the campus so he can use the computer labs. When they get to the university gate, she wields her white-lady magic and tells Alif to "look like a downtrodden migrant worker ... a rich woman's accessory" (141). Her sleight of hand, playing on the stereotypes of Gulf expat communities, is as successful as Vikram's riff on *Star Wars*, when he tells one of the State "thugs" that Dina and Alif "are not the *banu adam* you are looking for." Stereotypes create a kind of cultural blindness that can be manipulated for good or ill.

Even though The Convert is not a typical American, she remains within conventional narratives until she falls in love with Vikram. In the aftermath of the attack on the mosque, Vikram takes The Convert and Dina into the land of the jinn, where they find refuge in the palace of a *marid*, "a monster [with] ... an enormous torso topped by an improbably toothy head, skin shining darkly" (333). The Convert and Vikram marry, and she gets pregnant with his child, which the *marid*—after Vikram dies—takes as his responsibility, becoming a giant "fussy nursemaid." As a result of her union with Vikram, The Convert feels the world enlarge: "[T]he horizon has been pushed back and there's infinitely more between it and me than I once thought" (343). She has literally broken out of her epistemological frameworks—she's going to stay in the world of the jinn even after the baby is born—and her understanding of her faith is no longer expressed in rigid rules but in a sense of wonder and expansiveness. She points out that Vikram has never done anything "really blasphemous," and seems comfortable with the apparent paradox that the irreverent jinn might be devout.

Just as The Convert must put aside her conventional ways of looking at the world in favor of a more capacious awareness, so too must Alif. The Convert learns from Vikram, and Alif learns from what is to him an equally unlikely source: a member of the royal family. Convinced that all royals are corrupt, Alif is shocked when a prince in a spotless thobe comes into his prison cell, intent on rescuing him. The man introduces himself first by his online hacker handle, NewQuarter01, and then admits that his real name is Prince Abu Talib Al Mukhtar ibn Hamza. NewQuarter says he's twenty-sixth in line to the throne and describes himself as "one inbred bastard with a vendetta," intent on ridding The City of The Hand's tyranny. Using a version of The Convert's trick, NewQuarter flexes his privilege in front of the prison guards and hustles a disguised Bilal and Alif into the back of his BMW, which he uses for its anonymity—"all the princes drive them." The men escape, only to flip the car over in a sand dune and become stranded deep in the Empty Quarter, the vast stretch of Arabian Desert that reaches from the Emirates to Saudi Arabia. Despite the crash, Alif is overwhelmed with relief at escaping prison and begins to pray, "breathing inarticulate thanks." NewQuarter is horrified by the idea that Alif is praying without having performed the requisite ablutions. Earlier in the novel Bilal had chastised Alif for the same thing, but prison has changed Bilal's mind:

> I am not the state of my feet. I am not the dirt on my hands or the hygiene of my private parts. If I were these things, I would not have been at liberty to pray at any time since my arrest. But I did pray, because I am not these things. In the end, I am not even myself. I am a string of bones speaking the word *God*.
>
> (292)

The echo between "string of code" and "string of bones" links tech and body, faith and science, and offers another iteration of learning to see beyond simple assumptions. Alif's genuflections are actual experiences of faith, very different from his perfunctory utterances during prayers when he was younger. This expression of faith seems of a piece with Alif's realization, as they flee the prison, that they should be freeing everyone who is there: "[I]sn't this what we're meant to do? . . . Aren't we meant to believe in something?" Alif has never before thought about what his purpose might be, and he's never fully considered the needs of others before his own.

Alif's friendship with NewQuarter illustrates Alif's shifting outlook and helps him shake free of his binary way of thinking. NewQuarter, he realizes, is not a "fat idiot" prince, but someone who uses his privilege to dismantle unjust structures. He's bought a satellite dish rather than a "gold-plated Mercedes," because he knows that in the wars of the digital age, the winner will be "he who has a clean and reliable internet uplink. Censors be damned" (393). Even with his love of technology, NewQuarter (unlike Alif) does not dismiss the presence of jinn or acts of magic. The distinction between rational and nonrational, he suggests, is a Western concept, invented by "a bunch of European intellectuals in tights [who] decided to draw a line between what's rational and what's not . . . our ancestors [didn't think] the distinction was necessary" (369). Parceling ideas and concepts into rigid categories becomes a manifestation of an orientalizing impulse, a legacy of the nineteenth-century Enlightenment thinkers—men like Edward Lane and Richard Burton, translators and marketers of *The Arabian Nights*—who characterized "Arabia" as a place of exoticism and fantasy. Bilal agrees with NewQuarter and explains that "once upon a time, students of Islamic law were encouraged to give free rein to their imaginations." He gives Alif and NewQuarter the example of the ancient discussion about when a person needs to enter a state of ritual purity while traveling on the hajj:

> [I]f you were on foot, when? If you went by boat, when? ... and then one student ... posed the question: what if one were to fly? The proposition was taken as a serious exercise in the adaptability of the law. As a result, we had rules governing air travel during hajj five hundred years before the invention of the commercial jet.
>
> (369)

The layering of ideas that Bilal describes is what Alif tries to teach the computer: "multiple origin points, interrelated geneses, systems of multivalent cause and effect" (227). Alif comes to see the importance of multiplicity and engagement, the need to draw people in rather than push them out.

Engaging with a sense of wonder enables us, as readers, to connect ourselves to a larger whole and thus resist narratives that rest on facile binaries or narrow singularities. This sense of wonder also enables the sort of irony that Haraway describes: "the tension of holding incompatible things together because both or all are necessary and true. Irony is about humor and serious play. It is also a rhetorical strategy and a political method" (1991, "Science, Technology" 149). Her definition highlights the complexity of what Alif wants to teach a computer program to do: "think in metaphors ... [with] knowledge existing in several states simultaneously and without contradiction" (227). The final program that Alif writes operates in just this fashion: Every time he hits the "enter" key as he reprograms Tin Sari, he mutters *bismillah*, the first word in the Quran. He builds the program drawing equally on technology and faith. Alif holds Dina's hand as he types with his other hand and asks her to pray as he executes the program. Dina says "I'm not sure I can pray for a computer program," but she does so anyway, as does Alif. Faith and code, satellites and prayers—all come together to create something new, a way to root out absolutism, dogmatism, and tyranny.

Alif's blessed program gets released just as protests break out in The City, where people have been revolutionized by tyranny, just as Alif has. The Hand's efforts to police the internet have crashed the electrical grid (thus proving the necessity of owning one's own satellite), which seems to have been the crisis that finally sent people into the streets. The protesters are a polyglot group: "women bareheaded and veiled; old men in the red armbands of the Communist Party, men with beards and robes [carrying] signs and placards in Arabic, Urdu, English, Malay" (379). Their chants against the State's security apparatus and in favor of justice happen "in something less than unison," but their lack of unison doesn't matter. As Alif notes, "they're all marching together . . . all the disaffected scum." Dina, ever the astute reader, looks at the crowd and says "the emir is doomed" because she notices "the number of women in the streets. Last week it would have taken a forklift to get those same ladies out of their houses" (384). Alif is chagrined that people have begun to rebel because they can't access Facebook, but he feels an obligation to try and stop The Hand: Alif has developed a sense of purpose, precisely the thing that Lauren says fuels engagement with Earthseed.

Alif's newly developed skills as a reader allow him to defeat The Hand in their final showdown, which Alif presents as a coding challenge. He dares The Hand to "pick up [*Alf Yeom*], open it, and tell me how you would outcode me" (407). Alif knows that The Hand will not be able to tolerate the fluidity of the book, which cannot be controlled or interpreted by human intervention. The jinn magic that preserved the manuscript ensured that even if long-ago humans "never cracked the code [of the stories] themselves, the books would be vital and healthy for future generations, who might have more success" (208). The *Alf Yeom* becomes a version of "kids' stuff," the fantasy stories that Vikram explained were full of secret knowledge. It doesn't matter if we don't get all those ideas on our first reading: The book remains, vital and healthy, for us to return to again and again. The Hand cannot tolerate these layers of meaning, and when he sees the final story in the book, titled "The Fall of the Hand, or A Sad Case of Early Retirement," he is enraged. His fury prevents him from noticing that Alif's program has worked and that the electrical grid is coming back on. The magic of the shifting stories obscures the sound of "the mingled uproar of man and machine" that indicates electronic windows opening, enabling the "world [to] look into the square [of The City] through the eyes of a thousand news feeds and posts and uploaded videos, and witness the cost of change" (412). The Hand's repressive firewall has been breached; the multiple voices and experiences of The City can now be seen around the world and the world can join The City. The chokehold of a single story has been broken.

The optimism of this moment—Wilson finished the novel as the Arab Spring protests swept across Egypt and North Africa with promises of social and governmental reforms—now seems chimerical, like the smoke of a jinn vanishing from the scene. And yet for Alif's City, there is the sense that through the internet we might achieve a more global sense of citizenship—if, that is, we can manage to own our own satellites, as NewQuarter does. The "disaffected scum" catch The Hand and hang him from a lamppost, a violent action that Alif thinks has been spurred on by malevolent demons. The program that defeats The Hand is the product of collaboration—NewQuarter's tech, Dina's faith, and a bevy of jinn sent by the *marid* to protect them. This collaboration, a loose affiliative community, offers The City an opportunity to reimagine itself, which NewQuarter thinks confusing and exciting. He imagines that Alif will "probably be elected president or something . . . but wait—are we even having a democracy? I've got no idea what's going on" (425). Alif's program has created this space of possibility and change.

In the novel's denouement, Alif sees Intisar standing on the side of the road being harassed by brutes. She admits that she left him because she didn't want "sneaking around and not having nice things . . . I only know how to live one way" (428). That is precisely the problem: In only knowing how to live one way, Intisar and her ilk represent the past, a hierarchy that allows the wealthy to exploit people and resources with impunity. Intisar, despite having found the *Alf Yeom*, is revealed as a bad reader because she is sure that the texts of the world can only be interpreted according to one set of principles. Alif notices that she looks "haughty, like an imperious child who had been denied a treat" when she realizes that Alif would choose Dina, a "shabby Alexandrian," over her. Intisar is used to getting what she wants and cannot adapt to a narrative in which she is denied.

As Alif and Dina walk away, back to their shabby neighborhood, she asks him what the last story in *Alf Yeom* said. "Nothing we couldn't have written together," he tells her, in a comment that brings them together as collaborators, as equals. Fittingly, he realizes that they're standing on the street where the entire journey began, where "he had begun to be transformed by the story of himself." Dina calls him by his real name—Mohammad—stripping away the veil of his hacker handle, and Alif understands that he doesn't need to strip away Dina's veil in order to know the woman underneath. His structures of feeling have changed; he can even imagine himself being kinder to his mother and speaking to the maid "in complete sentences ... clean[ing] the dust from his own shoes" (270). Like Lauren Olamina, Alif comes to understand that the best stories are those that evolve with us.

When we become better readers, we are better able to embrace change and accept failure, both of which are key to creating less hierarchical communities. While there is no dogmatic portrayal of citizenship in these novels, there is nevertheless a strong link being made between reading and community. As Elisabeth Gruner reminds us, "literacy writ large clearly has an association with citizenship [and] the specific correlation of adolescent literacy with civic engagement, as with both economic viability and empathy, is one primarily of futurity: that is, if literacy is required to make good citizens, adolescence is the time when this will (or won't) happen" (14). Both Alif and Lauren write texts that run counter to the official stories of their societies and that integrate multiple levels of interpretation and awareness. The success of Alif's program rests on Dina's faith and on NewQuarter's satellite, an investment that highlights NewQuarter's own challenge to his society. Instead of buying gold-plated cars and other empty symbols of wealth, NewQuarter buys the technology to enable widespread communication: His satellite allows even the most marginalized voices to be heard. As we see in the example of Larkin, education alone will not automatically foster community or enable conversation; her advanced degree does not make her more receptive to marginalized voices or narratives that run counter to the fundamentalism of CA. The practice of cosmopolitanism requires people—as citizens, as readers—to bridge seemingly disparate modes of discourse and recognize the power of metaphor.

Notes

1. Butler wrote this novel, she said, in response to the Rodney King riots in Los Angeles.
2. The 1992 Earth Summit in Rio de Janeiro, Brazil, began the process that led to the Kyoto Protocols, which the United States did not endorse; the US also proved to be the sticking point in several other important agenda items, including an agreement to conserve biological diversity.
3. Butler's own work has been and continues to be incredibly "useful" both in terms of its prescience about our contemporary moment and for what it represents in the realm of speculative fiction, which has long been regarded as a bastion of whiteness. Butler, along with Samuel R. Delaney, opened the door for writers like N. K. Jemisin, Nnedi Okorafor, Ben Okri, and others.
4. In an interesting overlap with Wilson's novel, a "daemon" is also a computer program that runs in the background without user intervention.
5. Wilson uses the spelling "Quran," rather than "Qur'an" or "Koran." Intisar refers to "Djinn," but throughout the rest of the novel, Wilson uses the word "jinn" rather than "djinn." I have followed Wilson's usages throughout this book.
6. These layers of meaning may also resonate with the metaphoric language of sacred texts as feminist theologian Sandra Schneiders has defined it: "Genuine metaphor is not primarily a rhetorical decoration or an abbreviated comparison. It is a proposition (explicit or implied) constituted by an irresolvable tension between what it affirms (which is somehow true) and what it necessarily denies (namely, the literal truth of the assertion) . . . It forces the mind to reach toward meaning that exceeds or escapes effective literal expression" (qtd. in Gruner 136, citing Schneiders, "The Bible and Feminism" 38). Lyra Belacqua, in *The Golden Compass*, is described as reading her alethiometer in a similar state of mind, hovering across multiple meanings embedded in single images.

2

Loving the Monsters

This chapter is about mushrooms and bugs. Full disclosure: I am fond of mushrooms but I hate bugs. I'm afraid of them. This fear is probably due to the Midwestern summer I spent being chased around by my younger brother as he brandished a jar full of red-eyed locusts that he'd gathered from the swarms of seventeen-year cicadas inundating our suburban neighborhood. I can barely look at a cricket without flinching, and as for all those articles and books that extol insects and crustaceans as an almost infinitely renewable source of protein ... no. Lobsters in the shell terrify me; I can't even peel shrimp. Bugburgers are not in my future. I cannot find the strength to look beyond the absolute otherness of insects. They're tiny little monsters: Even innocuous creatures like ladybugs look strange when you get up close.

My fear makes it difficult to appreciate the point that Rosi Braidotti makes in *Nomadic Theory* that insects are "powerful indicators of the decentering of anthropocentrisms [that] point to posthuman sensibilities and sexualities" (105). Intellectually, I can appreciate her point. But my fear is such that I may never be able to get to that posthuman sensibility—and my failing, I think, is illustrative of a difficulty that rests in the center of cosmopolitan theory. How do we overcome disgust, move past concepts that repulse us on some deep and nonintellectual level? Braidotti suggests that our disgust about insects is in some sense irrelevant because they are rhetorically already embedded in our lives. The World Wide Web, innovations in molecular biology, and other technological inventions illustrate how insects have already become paradigmatic to our world, even as they horrify us. Insects embody contradiction: "attraction and repulsion, disgust and desire" (*Nomadic Theory* 104). We see this inseparable contradiction in *Storm of Locusts*, Rebecca Roanhorse's 2019 sequel to *Trail of Lightning*, which features a man who is also a swarm of locusts. He embodies yet another seeming opposition—the distinction between individual and group, solitary and swarm. Braidotti suggests that insects are "actualized slices of alternative living matter, which expresses the multiplicity of possible worlds and their copresence within our humanized universe. They are a radical form of otherness we cannot perceive, wrapped up as we are in our habits, which are the locus of our structural limitations" (102). Structural limitations come from our habits of mind, the ideological structures to which we are so often blind and that have led us to the point of Anthropocene collapse. One of these habits is the habit of monsterizing: the ease with which humans draw boundaries around themselves, sure of their own inherent centrality and the disposability of Others. I am, sadly, all too willing to smash a bug if I find it in my house (although I try not to kill spiders, unless they are actively crawling on me): Bugs are monsters and thus, to me, disposable. And yet I am willing to concede that seeing bugs as disposable may in fact make *me* the monster, not the hapless cricket crawling up from my kitchen drain.

In order to unwrap our habits of mind and reimagine the relationship between human and planet, we need to shift our structures of feeling, which is of course made more complicated if one of those feelings is revulsion. My feelings about bugs remain more or less unchanged—I still flinch when I see a cockroach—but I am willing to concede that my fear is irrational. I will probably never knowingly (or willingly) eat a bug-burger, but as Appiah points out in his discussion about disgust, I can understand the need for eating such things even if I don't agree with it: "[U]nderstanding one another may be hard; it can certainly be interesting. But it doesn't require that we come to agreement" (*Cosmopolitanism* 78). Changing our structures of feeling, that is to say, may lead to a realignment of the sorts of structural limitations that Braidotti refers to—and that, for many of us, are essentially invisible. We like to believe that we ourselves are free of ideological constraints: Only other people fall prey to such things, we think. Fiction, particularly speculative fiction, can show us the ways in which we are all wrapped in ideological structures—and how we might detangle ourselves from those webs. Writing several decades after Williams, but in a style imbued with a similar Marxist aesthetic, Gloria Anzaldúa writes in *Borderlands/La Frontera* (1987, 2012) that "nothing happens in the 'real' world unless it first happens in the images in our heads" (109). The novels I discuss in this chapter—Rebecca Roan-horse's *Trail of Lightning* (2018) and *Storm of Locusts* (2019) and Nancy Farmer's duology, *The House of Scorpion* (2002) and *The Lord of Opium* (2013)—are set in Anzaldúa's borderlands and show us what happens when we attempt to reinterpret not only the geography, but also the very idea of "the human."

At the center of their speculative dystopian fictions, both Roanhorse and Farmer position a monstrous "Other," a figure that calls attention to our contemporary moment and asks us to consider whether the monster is always something (or someone) to be feared. These novels suggest that we can affiliate with those who are unlike us and that the monsters we most have to fear are the monsters who see the world solely in terms of commodity. Roanhorse and Farmer illustrate the causal link between monsters and climate catastrophe. Landscapes can be exploited and destroyed when those who inhabit these ge-ographies are seen as lesser, as other, as monster. It's the argument of Rob Nixon's *Slow Violence and the Environmentalism of the Poor* (2011), which examines the ways in which capitalism destroys the landscapes inhabited by impoverished and marginalized peoples, who are often displaced as a result of harmful environmental practices—thus lead-ing to further disenfranchisement and worsening social conditions. Nixon theorizes what these novels demonstrate: The enforcement of national boundaries and an emphasis on profit margins lead to the marginalization and othering of any entity that gets in the way. Over *there* are monsters—depraved, dirty, violent, ignorant, uncivilized—and *we*, over here, are humans: civilized, rational, and entitled to any resources we desire.

The boundaries between "us" and "them" create distance and fear, as does the fear that if the boundaries collapse, we may no longer be able to recognize ourselves. What if "they" are just like us? In Bram Stoker's *Dracula* (1897), for instance, the moment that most chills Jonathan Harker after he's escaped from Count Dracula's castle is when he sees the Count in a London street on a busy afternoon, as if he were just another human. It is this fear that makes clones such a potent threat in popular culture, as Erin Newcomb points out in her discussion of Farmer's books: "[W]hat if humans aren't that unique or special . . . the clone walking unknown in our midst challenges the very notion of human uniqueness and leads to speculations about what

actually makes up a human identity" (178). Farmer puts a clone—
Matt Alacran—at the center of her duology, while Roanhorse creates
a protagonist, Maggie Hoskie, a Diné (Navajo) who looks like a normal
human but has "clan powers" that seem monstrous to those around
her.[1] These novels are set in what had been the Southwestern United
States, but in the future worlds of both books, the maps have been
radically redrawn by the destructive twin engines of nationalism and
capitalism. Even in these future worlds, however, Matt and Maggie
are seen as threats because they do not fit neatly into any category.

These novels dramatize a cosmopolitan critique of US identity politics, while demonstrating the need for a more expansive cosmopolitan
theory that can better accommodate both feminism and the idea of
nonhuman agency. Roanhorse, who is of mixed African American
and Native (Ohkay Owingeh Pueblo) descent, says that she wrote *Trail
of Lightning* in order to create a book that she wanted to read: "a science fiction and fantasy story where Native characters held front and
center, where the landscape was filled with the places and the people
that I knew from living on the rez, where the gods and heroes were
of North American Indigenous origin" ("Interview" np). Both sets of
novels illustrate what Liz Thiel and Alison Waller have called the ability of YA fiction to "engender and perpetuate new ideologies" (3).
The novels I discuss in this chapter offer these "new ideologies"
through sustained engagements with questions about female agency,
environmental stewardship, and the nature of home.

Neither Maggie nor Matt embodies the usual American hero, the
unencumbered (male) protagonist who is so central to America's myth
about itself. Instead the novels demonstrate the need for affiliation,
for kinship groups that embrace rather than ostracize monstrosity.
The monsters don't disappear; they are not "cured." They are, instead, loved. Kinship—a volitional affiliation that is not predicated
on biology or obligation—becomes the key to creating resistance not
only to the ravages of capitalism but also to the Western and solip-
sistic emphasis on individualism. We may not necessarily end up in a
hive, like bees, or a leaderless swarm, like locusts, but when we create affiliative communities that are not threatened by monstrosity, we
can begin to reimagine the structures of feeling with which we relate
to the planet. Marleena Mustola and Sanna Karkulehto, in an essay
about monsters in picture books, note that "children . . . are always

positioned as 'others' in a world where the adult perspective is the perpetual default [and] ... monsters could ... offer ways in which to explore and reconfigure the ethical relationships between humans and nonhumans" (126). What these novels show us is that we shouldn't fear "them," but rather the systems that manipulate us into thinking that way: The real monsters are those who think only in terms of commodity and domination.

Section One: The Sixth World

In the aftermath of a series of climate catastrophes that have radically altered the geography of North America, Maggie Hoskie becomes acquainted with her monstrous powers and in the process discovers the power of community. As a result of her magical nonhuman development, Maggie finds new ways to engage with the world around her, a complex and ongoing process that will extend into the other books in the series. Her struggles illustrate new ideologies in which we can see possibilities for how we might redefine "the local" and how we might exist in a post-national world.

The post-apocalyptic landscape of Roanhorse's "Sixth World" novels literalizes the consequences of unchecked resource exploitation and suggests that in the face of climate catastrophe, national boundaries are irrelevant. *Trail of Lightning* seems of a piece with other YA speculative fictions that imagine redrawn worlds, such as Panem in Suzanne Collins's "The Hunger Games" series (2008–2010); the watery worlds of New Mungo in Julie Bertagna's *Exodus* (2002); the post-apocalyptic New Pretty Town in Scott Westerfeld's "Uglies" series (2005–2007). The worlds of these novels offer "the possibility not only of critiquing everything that has gone wrong with humanist society, but also that of providing a way forward ... a revision or reimagining" (Harrison 11). Roanhorse has said that she didn't conceive of her book as YA, but "there is some excellent Fantasy being written right now in YA, so perhaps we should stop using YA as a way to dismiss women SFF [science fiction and fantasy] writers and see it as a compliment to our creativity" ("Interview" np).[2] When we read these novels, we are given the opportunity to re-envision our own worlds and our role in those worlds: What forms of agency might we find if we allow ourselves to think beyond the circumscribed confines of our social structures?

In *Trail of Lightning*, the first book of the "Sixth World" series, Maggie struggles to understand her clan powers and why she has been abandoned by Neizghání, the god who had taken her on as an apprentice. Called a monster by her community because of her clan powers, Maggie must use those same powers to kill a monster created by a clever and violent witch, Ma'ii, who wants Maggie to give in to her most violent tendencies and thus turn her into his personal assassin. In the process of hunting down this monster, Maggie befriends Kai Arviso, who also has clan powers and may in fact be an immortal. The second book, *Storm of Locusts*, picks up immediately where the first book left off, when Maggie finds herself in the unlikely position of being a surrogate aunt to Ben, a young girl whose traumas have also unleashed clan powers. In addition to tending to Ben, Maggie must stop a man who calls himself the White Locust and wants to erase the Diné from the earth.

Maggie's world may seem, at least initially, quite familiar: a Navajo reservation in the American Southwest where people barely eke out a living and violent death is a fact of life. According to a recent study from the National Congress of American Indians (nd), the rate of suicide among Native American populations is 2.5 times higher than in the rest of the United States; four in five Native women will experience violent crime; education rates are lower than in the rest of the United States. Hardships like these exist in Maggie's world—except "there is no United States left" (*Trail of Lightning* 74). A flood that is known as the Big Water "drowned most of the world" and now the western coastline stretches from "San Antonio [Texas] to Sioux Falls [South Dakota]." Roanhorse has said that she set her novel in the future because "Natives are so often relegated to the past, when we are still here and will continue to be here in the future" (Coleman np). There is no harkening back to some primordial innocence in these novels; instead, Roanhorse weaves together Native American lore and tradition with high-octane fantasy in a way that engages readers at the level of plot while offering an indictment of Anglo-European environmental attitudes that led to "the Earth herself stepp[ing] in and drown[ing] them all" (*Trail of Lightning* 54) which is how Maggie thinks about the flood that destroyed the continent when she was fifteen.

Innocent people are drowned in the cataclysm, but so too are the multinational corporations with private armies that build oil pipelines, destroy habitats and sacred ground with fracking, and gobble up land, literally "shaking the bedrock with their greed" (*Trail of Lightning* 22). The multinationals may have been destroyed, but there are still those who see natural resources as a source of wealth, such as the water barons who live in the Buque (formerly Albuquerque). The water barons "control everything. Deep wells and waterworks ... catchments and evaporators up in the mountains. Water making them wealthy like Renaissance princes" (54). Hoarding water is one reason that the Dinétah land suffers from a drought, even in the aftermath of the floods, which for the most part left Dinétah land untouched. The land was preserved by a Wall, built when Maggie was young, during the Energy Wars. When the Wall was proposed, many people in the tribe said it was "a paranoid attempt at border control ... just like the Wall [that] the doomed American government tried to build along its Southern border" (22). Proponents of the Wall insist that it will protect them against "conquest, manifest destiny"—protect them, that is to say, from history and its legacies. The Wall survives the floods for reasons that are similar to the way that Alif's coding successfully brings down The Hand. Just as Alif mutters *bismillah* at the end of each line of code and asks Dina to pray, so too with "every lath" of the Wall, "a blessing [is] given ... the Wall took on a life of its own" (22). The novel suggests that there is strength in the union of faith and technology, in setting old-world beliefs into new contexts.

Maggie appreciates the beauty of the Wall and the fact that it withstood the floodwaters, but she also realizes—as demonstrated by the water barons—that "sometimes the worst monsters are inside" (22). The alluring beauty of the Wall, which gleams with shell, abalone, turquoise, and jet, seems like a testament of all that is good and pure about the Diné. But its beauty does not necessarily mean the people are safe. Maggie fears the vigilantes known as the Law Dogs, "a pack of bullies with badges," for example, and she knows that as a woman living alone—even one with clan powers—she is vulnerable. Being Diné is important to her, but it does not seem to her a guarantee of anything. Maggie seems to understand what Bryan S. Turner argues in "Cosmopolitan Virtue" (2002): "[O]ur modern dilemmas cannot be solved simply by a naïve return to origins" (58). Her awareness becomes particularly important in *Storm of Locusts*, when her opponent is a man who preaches about the salvation to be found through a fundamentalist return to origins, a seductive narrative that creates a cultish acceptance of violence and destruction.

Maggie doesn't fit into any of the narratives used by those around her to explain their world: "I'm human," Maggie says, "a five-fingered girl. But I'm not exactly normal" (*Trail of Lightning* 6). She is not normal because she has powers that come from her clans—the "Walks-Around" clan gives her the ability to move "faster than human[s]" (58) and the power of the Living Arrow clan means that she is "really good at killing people" (59). Her powers set her apart from the rest of the Diné, who are "five-fingered" but without extra-human powers (6). The people around Maggie "hate [her]" (4) because "she's not right . . . she's wrong, Navajo way" (5). Even in a context that allows for sentience in the nonhuman world, Maggie is a threat because she collapses distinctions between spirit and mortal, monster and human, irrational and rational.

Maggie roots herself in a specific tradition, but she realizes that those traditions will be impacted by the changing world around her. She is not nostalgic for some more "authentic" Diné moment. Her "local" has been radically and irrevocably altered. Roanhorse said that in these novels she wanted to give her Diné readers "a chance to see themselves accurately portrayed and centered in Fantasy. There are so many Easter eggs in the book if you're from the Window Rock/Gallup area, and I've put those in the book for Navajo readers to enjoy and laugh at" (Roanhorse, "Interview" np). Along with local "Easter eggs," references in these novels come from an array of sources, both ancient and contemporary, reminding us that to be "Native" is not to be stuck in the past. At a climactic moment in a traditional ceremony, Kai wishes he'd had some duct tape; Kai wears a variety of heavy metal t-shirts (AC/DC and Metallica are in regular rotation); Ma'ii, who is the trickster figure Coyote, hides his animal body in the clothes of a "gentleman scoundrel from some old Hollywood Western" (*Trail of Lightning* 87); and when Maggie and Kai are on the run from a variety of bad guys, they find refuge at the "All-American Bar" (153), a drinking establishment named for something that no longer exists. Maggie has retrofitted her truck to run on "hooch" because gasoline is "hard to come by," an ironic inversion of US history: The alcohol that once devastated Native American communities now powers Maggie's truck, so that she is mobile, while most of Anglo America is gone.

The Big Water may have washed away "America," but Diné history has not been entirely lost, as Kai discovers when he and Maggie search an abandoned library. Maggie says she's never been much of a library person, but she nonetheless recognizes the value of what she and Kai find: "oral histories. Knowledge from elders about their lives, their time in residential schools, stories of parents who survived the Long Walk . . . Navajo scholars were afraid we'd lose the knowledge when the elders passed" (69). The recordings preserve a legacy of US governmental oppression, a detail that grounds this speculative fantasy in the real, forcing us to ask whether the horrors of Native American history are any more or less unbelievable than the world in which Kai and Maggie live.

Maggie's situation offers an example of how "the local" may not always be the source of strength that Appiah and other (male) theorizers of cosmopolitanism think it is. The water barons, Law Dogs, and Diné deities are all local, and in their different ways, they are all more monstrous than Maggie because they see the world purely in terms of resources for their own consumption. The attack that results in Maggie's clan powers being unleashed for the first time, for example, occurs (although Maggie does not know it until the conclusion of the novel) because Coyote/Ma'ii wants to force Maggie into becoming a killer and murders Maggie's grandmother in order to make that happen. Appearing to Maggie as a fearsome witch, Coyote forces Maggie to cut her own grandmother's throat and then seems about to rape her: He knocks her to the ground and she feels a "fleshy hand scrape across [her] face" (106). At that moment, the adrenaline of clan power surges through her body and she fights back against her attackers, killing them all. In the aftermath she is stunned to discover "how terrible [she] could be" (109). Maggie's retaliatory murders turn her into a kind of vigilante, "the person you hire when the heroes have already come home in body bags" (*Trail of Lightning* 2). On the local level, the violence against Maggie and her grandmother reflects an all-too-common truth about life on reservations across the United States, where the rates of violence against women are significantly higher than elsewhere in the country.[3] The trauma of the attack unleashes Maggie's power but the ostracism she experiences as a result of becoming the monsterslayer may also speak to the treatment many women suffer when they dare to resist the violence of powerful men.

Sure that she is a freak, Maggie is surprised when Tah, an old medicine man, takes her under his wing, apparently unafraid of her violent nature. She and Tah "aren't even in the same clan, but he calls [her] daughter [and] that means something" (25). He accepts her nonhuman nature as part of the natural world, something to be acknowledged rather than despised. What develops, over the course of the two novels, is a kinship group of the sort that Donna Haraway imagines as an alternative to the tyranny of biological imperatives: "[W]e need to encourage . . . policies that engage scary demographic issues by proliferating other-than-natal kin" ("Anthropocene, Capitalocene" 164). The members of the kinship group that coheres around Maggie are not biologically connected, but they choose to affiliate, to find ways to connect across difference. Maggie's monstrous nature never goes away, but she is still woven into the affiliative connections that help her imagine a world where "life can be creat[ed] and sustain[ed]" (*Trail of Lightning* 36). It's important to note here that Maggie is thinking about the landscape, not childbirth. By the end of the second novel, Maggie's decrepit trailer and Tah's newly built hogan become the site of a Keshmish celebration that will be attended by this new kinship group, including mixed-race non-Native twins; Diné from different clans; a demi-god; several mortal bikers; and a mixed-race human with permanently attached metallic locust wings.[4]

Gideon, Maggie's antagonist in *Storm of Locusts*, resembles her in crucial ways: He is another "five-fingered" person who has suffered a near-death experience that releases latent clan powers. In his case, the transformation occurs when he is staked to the ground and swarmed by locusts: "[T]hey [came] out of the ground. Insects. Hundreds of them . . . biting me . . . eating me alive . . . a locust crawled into my mouth . . . and I couldn't stop it. I could feel its feet on my tongue, the flutter of its wings against my teeth" (298). Roanhorse says she chose locusts because "they creep me out" (Coleman np), and it is indeed difficult to read this description without a shudder. Gideon survives this trauma by deciding that the locusts could liberate him, "eat away that which was rotted and old and make way for the new [if] I just had the will, the desire, the goddamn *fortitude* to persevere" (*Storm of Locusts* 298). The clan powers revealed by this traumatic experience include the ability to bend metal and to shape-shift: Gideon can dissolve his human form into a swarm of locusts. In an important connection to Braidotti's theoretical ideas, Gideon also invests his followers with the ability to create a locust song that brings singer and listener into a state of "something fragile and beautiful . . . seductive" (22). Braidotti points out that the sounds insects make are "a real challenge for humanity [because] insect sound is instrumental . . . molecular and yet at the same time, the soundscapes they produce are pervasive . . . intimate . . . [and] collective" (*Nomadic Theory* 106). Gideon's noises are not designed to create a positive collective experience but, instead, the hypnotic noises made by Gideon's human-insect swarm become an aural weapon: "the song of nightmares long buried underneath the ground, the cry of a million hungry mouths" (80). Linking starvation with the sound of locusts suggests that Gideon's rage comes not only from his perceived slights at the hands of the Diné, but also from a long-simmering rage at the US government's genocidal treatment of the Native Americans.

Gideon's abilities erase the distinction between human and nonhuman, but his real monstrosity emerges in the fundamentalist simplicity with which he looks at the world. Disregarding the ambiguity of his own body, which is both insect and human, swarm and individual, Gideon—calling himself the White Locust—preaches a single story to his followers about their purity and the corruption of everyone else. His followers prove their devotion by allowing him to attach locust wings to their shoulders; they are seduced by his promise of creating a new beginning in which they will inherit the earth. Like the members of Christian America in Butler's *Parable of the Talents*, Gideon's followers are unwilling and unable to see anything outside of the narrative that Gideon offers them. The novels illustrate the destructive allure of narratives that operate along simple binaries and that preclude any attempts at connecting across the dividing lines.

Gideon seems to offer his followers a sense of purpose, which is what Butler's Lauren Olamina offers the members of Earthseed, but where Earthseed's purpose is omnidirectional and generative, Gideon's is singular and destructive. He tries to recruit Maggie to support his vision by saying that the trauma of their emerging clan powers makes them similar, as does the fact that they've both been ostracized by the Diné as a result of their powers. If Maggie were to join him, he says, he could "help [her] find the one thing that eludes you . . . purpose. Isn't that what you need?" (255). What looks like an attempt at empathy, however, is actually an attempt to control Maggie's murderous abilities; Gideon is interested only in dominance, not conversation. Maggie tells him that "Dinétah is a place just like any other, with bad and good," but Gideon doesn't care. He plans to challenge the gods to "go forth to devour . . . remake the known world and bring the very gods to account" (261). The power of the locusts to "reorder entire landscapes" now belongs to him. He will use this power not in the service of a Braidotti-esque "decentering of anthropocentrisms [and] posthuman sensibilities" but in the service of vengeance and supremacy.

Gideon's human-locust body is both horrifying and beautiful, as if to further signify the temptation embedded in his plan to sweep the earth clean. For himself and his followers, he makes "giant locust wings made of flexible metal . . . as delicate and beautiful as lace" (259), but this beauty comes with a threat. He and his followers will fly to the Glen Canyon dam and plant explosives midway down the dam walls—a spot only accessible from the air. They plan to explode the walls of the megadam and wash away what Gideon claims is a corrupt society. His search for a single unifying narrative, paradoxically attainable only through hybridization, will erase everything else. While Gideon cloaks his plan in the rhetoric of ancient legends—the locust as a messenger of the gods, an emblem of transformation—his actions parallel the actions of the multinational corporations who created the devastation that led to the Big Water. In neither instance do the destroyers recognize the importance of those who will be destroyed, whether human or nonhuman. It is not his union with insects that makes Gideon a monster, but rather his willingness to use people as instruments in his monomaniacal quest.

Initially, Maggie and her companions do not take Gideon's plan seriously, but they have not taken into account the deeply embedded changes created by human interventions. They think that if the dam is breached, the water will find its natural course again as part of the Colorado River, and all will be well. Aaron, Gideon's foster brother, tells them they're wrong: "[T]he landscape [has] been permanently changed [and cannot handle] the destructive force of flowing water" (266). Glen Canyon dam holds "twenty-seven million acre feet" of water (an acre foot means enough water to cover an acre of land with a foot deep of water), which means that blowing up the dam would finish what the Big Water started. With his plan, Gideon will effectively "create his own natural disaster" (266). While most scientists and environmentalists agree that megadams have done more harm than good, there is no easy way to dismantle a large dam: The environmental damage has become part of the landscape.

What Gideon and his swarm of human-locust followers intend to do is a twenty-first-century version of Edward Abbey's 1975 novel *The Monkeywrench Gang*. In Abbey's novel, four hapless men sabotage as many environmentally destructive "development" projects as they can; they fantasize about blowing up the Glen Canyon dam but never do. Their fictional actions inspired the group Earth First to unfurl a 300-foot black polyurethane "crack" across the face of the dam in 1981, setting off a national panic. Maggie and her companions are thus in a paradoxical position: They must stop Gideon from causing another natural disaster by preventing him from destroying a long-standing symbol of environmental destruction and exploitation. Gideon's plan would be cataclysmic, but it would give the world a fresh start—one with far fewer humans in it. It would be the sort of disaster that Margaret Atwood imagines in *Oryx and Crake* (2003), when a scientist deliberately infects the world populations with a fatal disease in order to push reset on humanity.

A fresh start for humanity cannot occur without massive upheaval, as Roanhorse's *Storm of Locusts* makes clear. There is no possibility, despite what Gideon says, of returning to some idealized past or establishing a future devoid of contamination. The "Sixth World" books do not valorize the rhetoric of authenticity and purity that is so often found in eco-fiction and ecocriticism. Nixon criticizes the way ecocritics talk about "the authentic landscape" and the "virgin wilderness . . . [and] an ethics of place." He advocates for "bioregionalism," which he sees as being "responsive to natural characteristics rather than arbitrary administrative boundaries" (Nixon 238). Gideon, for all that he wants to destroy the Dinétah, also fetishizes it; he believes that after they blow up the dam, they will be able to achieve some sort of primordial innocence. But a return to innocence, as US environmentalist and writer Alex Steffen points out, is impossible: "[A] restoration of continuity has failed before it starts" ("We're Not yet Ready" np). Gideon does not address climate change directly, but his belief that somehow he can restore purity and authenticity to the world while ignoring the consequences of the Big Water is a fallacy. He doesn't understand, as Maggie does, the nature of contagion and contamination; she knows that there isn't anything that hasn't been influenced by something else and that there can be no return to innocence.

Gideon's new world order is predicated on his willingness to see other creatures as expendable, disposable. He also ignores the logic of the swarm: Locusts do not have a central leader. It is his insistence on being the individual ruler that proves to be his undoing, and why he is defeated through the collaborative efforts of Maggie and her companions—efforts that rely on ancient traditions and contemporary methods. When Kai comments on the ritual he performed to manipulate the weather against Gideon, he says he used "magic, [clan] medicine, science, and a little luck. If I had duct tape, I'd throw that in too" (*Storm of Locusts* 285). Maggie and Kai, wearing a Metallica t-shirt, bring together all the elements of their world, past and present. Their ideas about "authenticity" are fluid; we might say that in their ability to evolve with circumstance, Kai and Maggie demonstrate how structures of feeling can create material change. They join ancient landscapes and ancient gods with heavy metal music, duct tape, and retrofitted trucks. This ability to accept mixing and change also explains why none of Maggie's companions reject Caleb Goodacre, who is rescued from the swarm but decides to keep his wings because "he is still not convinced that Gideon was all wrong" (308).

The novel leaves open that question: Is Gideon wrong to believe that the rivers should be undammed? Is he wrong that the Diné can be exclusionary and xenophobic? And is he wrong to see the locusts as a model for future societies? The leaderless locusts, resilient and resourceful, powerful as a collective and vulnerable when they're isolated, highlight a social organism that is fluid and nonhierarchical, responsive to their local environment. The hallmarks of the locust swarm are also, and not uncoincidentally, the hallmarks of the affiliative community that has formed by the time the novel reaches its conclusion: fluid, nonhierarchical, responsive, rooted in the local but connected to the global.

The presence of the locusts in this novel help us to see a model of social organization that moves away from hierarchy. The locusts are not themselves monstrous; it is the way that Gideon has weaponized them that creates the problem.[5] When we realize that not all "monsters" are in fact monstrous, when we find ways to embrace rather than divide, we come closer to what Braidotti encourages us to think about: An "ethical approach based on posthumanist values, or on biocentered egalitarianism . . . critiques individualism and attempts to think about the interconnection of human and nonhuman agents" (*Nomadic Theory* 113). The monster is not the nonhuman; the monstrous is that which treats any entity as a commodity.

Section Two: *The House of Scorpion* and *The Lord of Opium*

Another organic nonhuman symbol of social reorganization emerges from underground in Nancy Farmer's borderlands duology, *The House of Scorpion* and *The Lord of Opium*: mushrooms. Mushrooms—mycelia—spread rhizomatically and, in addition to being edible, can also detoxify the soil. Farmer's novels, although quite different in their presentation of monsters and climate catastrophe, come to a conclusion similar to Roanhorse's books: Our future societies stand a better chance of survival if we can establish affiliative communities and nonbiological kinship groups, as well as realign our human relationship to the planet.

In the world of Farmer's novels, distinctions are made between humans and clones, with the latter regarded as livestock that are monstrous but necessary, because they serve as biologically perfect organ donors.[6] Matt Alacran, the hero of these two novels, has been grown in the belly of a cow to serve as an organ donor for the wealthy drug lord once known as Matteo Alacran and now called El Patrón. El Patrón's fiefdom is the land of Opium, situated between the United States and Mexico (called Aztlán) and extending west to the Pacific coast. Opium is comprised of several different drug farms and its borders are maintained by a force field whose energy source resides in the Scorpion Star, a sort of Death Star satellite that hovers over the country. The country is both technologically advanced—there are clones and microchipped servants called eejits—and rustic: El Patrón insists that his estate be run as if it's still the mid-nineteenth century, so there is no air conditioning or electricity (unless he's having guests from outside Opium). In Book One, Matt discovers that he is destined for organ harvesting and escapes, hoping to find refuge in Aztlán with a girl named Maria Mendoza, who had been kind to him when she visited the estate; in Book Two, Matt becomes the ruler of Opium after El Patrón's death and must figure out how to avoid becoming a tyrant like his genetic precursor while also keeping Opium safe from other drug lords and Maria's mother, a zealot who wants to achieve her virtuous goals by any means necessary.

By virtue of its geographic setting, the story of Matt's trajectory from livestock-clone to the ruler of Opium sheds light on the fraught nature of the border between the United States and Mexico. The things that Farmer imagines, which may have seemed impossible at the time of her writing, now seem much closer to the realm of the real in the aftermath of the Trump administration's treatment of refugees, particularly children. As Lysa Rivera writes in an article about neoliberalism and dystopias, "[B]orderlands dystopias confront not only the near and distant futures, but also how the histories of U.S.-Mexico colonial and neocolonial relations of power have provided and continue to provide the material conditions for this future" ("Neoliberalism and Dystopia" 294). Matt's fate offers us the opportunity to consider how best to dismantle an unjust system, even as his journey also puts a post-human spin on the Enlightenment question about the relative influences of nature and nurture on individual lives. I use "relative" here quite deliberately: As a clone, Matt's only biological relative is El Patrón, which means that Matt's nature is precisely that of the 143-year-old sadistic tyrant. Over the course of the two books, Matt acquires another set of relatives: the group of disparate people who choose to affiliate themselves with him, regardless of his status as a clone, and who help him dismantle El Patrón's empire. The fate of the country entwines with Matt's, in that if Matt can resist the genetic impulse of El Patrón's tyranny, he can find alternative methods of governing the country. Matt-the-clone is regarded as a monster, and the property of another monster, a tyrant who governs a monstrosity of an empire. Matt must learn how to dismantle the empire and its monsters, a particularly difficult task given that El Patrón's voice echoes in Matt's head even after his death, in a constant attempt to dictate Matt's behavior.

Matt and other clones are seen as beasts, and as a result of their nonhuman status, they can be exploited with impunity. As a young child, Matt doesn't understand why he is kept separate from everyone else on El Patrón's estate. He knows only that his caretaker, Celia, is not his mother and that she works as a cook in El Patrón's kitchens. When the spoiled nieces and nephews of El Patrón find Celia's cottage and Matt inside it, they know immediately who—or what—Matt is because of the tattoo on the sole of his foot, which reads "Property of Alacran estate" (*House of Scorpion* 23). The children, aided by a servant named Rosa, refer to Matt as "it"; they take him from Celia, lock him in a room carpeted in sawdust, and make him eat from bowls without utensils so that he has to "put his face in the bowl like a dog" (40). After Matt cuts his foot on broken glass, his cell is carpeted with even deeper litter: Rosa tells the doctor that it's healthier for "the beast," referring to practices they use to keep "chickens healthy . . . their filth settles to the bottom [and] it saves their feet from getting infected" (42). Treated as a beast, Matt loses his ability to speak, which those around him see as further evidence that he is less than human.

El Patrón and Celia both call Matt *mi vida*, but El Patrón means it literally: Matt's organs will be used to prolong El Patrón's already extraordinarily long life. Matt is being raised for slaughter, and when El Patrón punishes Rosa for her treatment of Matt, it isn't out of a sense of justice or concern for Matt, it's narcissism: Matt is "the most important person in [his] life," El Patrón tells his family and staff after Matt has been brought from the animal pens to El Patrón's mansion: "He is to be educated, well-fed, and entertained" (62). Ironically, Matt is the only person who doesn't understand the real reason for his privileged treatment or the reality of El Patrón's brutal regime. Matt sees El Patrón as a folk hero, a man who when he was a child had to scrabble for pesos thrown on the ground by a wealthy rancher and then became the absolute ruler of an entire country. Only when Matt shakes free of this myth will he have a chance to become the sort of leader who can effectively reimagine the structures of his society so that they are more just—and more attuned to the rhythms of the planet itself. He must unwrap himself from El Patrón's habit of seeing everything around him as a commodity.

Theories of cosmopolitanism rest on the idea that, as Lauren Olamina says, everyone has something to offer. Appiah has the same idea: "[E]verybody matters: that is our central idea" (*Cosmopolitanism* 144). El Patrón perverts this idea: Matt "matters" to him, but not in the right way. In the eyes of El Patrón's family and all the other non-microchipped humans, anything nonbiological is impure and thus commodifiable. And thus, despite the fact that Matt is genetically all Alacran and all Mexican, he is seen as impure because he has been produced nonbiologically. His story demonstrates what Zoe Jaques notes in *Children's Literature and the Posthuman* (2015): "[C]hildren's fiction offers a heretofore neglected resource for understanding cultures of the human and nonhuman, and often questions the nature, parameter, and dominion of humanity" (6). The question of what makes someone "human" runs through Farmer's duology, as does her answer: "[H]uman" is a term that is socially determined. Matt believes that it is "the natural order of things" for humans to hate clones but, as he comes to learn, "natural order" is in fact created by a system of unjust laws and social manipulation (*House of Scorpion* 275). The myths and legends that circulate through Opium maintain El Patrón's power by perpetuating the idea that it is natural for some bodies to be abject and monstrous, and that to challenge that status is to risk a terrible fate. When Matt is sent to a labor camp inhabited by young orphan boys, for example, the boys insist that there is no country called Opium, only a place called "Dreamland," which is ruled over by a vampire king who, if he catches you, will turn you into a zombie slave. Like most horror stories, this one has elements of truth: El Patrón is a vampire, sucking the life out of his clones and out of the earth itself in an effort to prolong both life and profit. Better to stay in the labor camp than to risk being turned into a zombie—a nonhuman. The post-apocalyptic setting of the novel, combined with El Patrón's advanced age and rapaciousness, illustrates the consequences of what Braidotti calls a "vampirelike economic system . . . based on stock and exchange, common standards and unjust distribution; accumulation and profit" (*Nomadic Theory* 113).

Matt's status as a piece of precious property has kept him innocent about the world outside El Patrón's estate; when he arrives in the labor camp, he is initially delighted to have found children his own age and thinks he's found "the biggest and best oasis in the world." His journey is like that of Pinocchio, who in his quest to become a "real boy" is tricked into going to Pleasure Island, where all the children are eventually turned into donkeys and sold. The labor camp is not an oasis, of course, but its antithesis: a factory set in the middle of a blasted landscape that cannot sustain life. Matt and the other boys work at a plankton factory near what once was the Gulf of California but is now a narrow, fetid channel whose banks are littered with the mammoth skeletons of whales. The boys harvest plankton, which one guard says is "delicious, nutritious, the most delicious dish in the world" (*House of Scorpion* 281). The guards don't mention that they don't eat the plankton-based food that is slopped out to the boys and tastes like "rancid glue" (281). Chacho, one of the boys who befriends Matt, offers his own assessment of Aztlán's labor policies: The boys are "part of the crotting production of resources for the crotting good of the people" (281). The boys are cogs in the machine of plankton extraction; they sieve the plankton out of vast tanks while trying to avoid the toxic water in which the plankton float. The labor camp is set among vast salt flats and sand dunes, all of which were created as a result of what one of the guards calls the "great engineering triumph of Aztlán." This "triumph" is a huge pipe that diverts the Colorado River underground so that it no longer feeds into the Gulf of Mexico. The guard's delight at this environmental manipulation highlights the all-too-human tendency to find glory in domination over the natural world. As a result of this engineering feat, the Gulf has all but dried up and the river has become an underground canal that supplies water to Opium. The whales that used to populate the Gulf are dead, but that fact doesn't bother Matt. In an indication that he has not yet broken free of his genetic precursor, all Matt can see is that Opium gets irrigated for free and reflects that "El Patrón loved a bargain" (281). Farmer's novels illustrate the real cost of such "bargains," in terms of both human life and planet life: Monsters are those who exploit and commodify resources. What really is "for the good of the people"?

Matt doesn't see the cost of El Patrón's bargains because he is still enmeshed in the narrative that posits El Patrón as a rags-to-riches hero, a savior who triumphed over adversity. Tam Lin, El Patrón's bodyguard, who has tried to educate Matt about the realities of his world, gives Matt a pamphlet about the history of Opium, in which Matt reads about his genetic parent. The book explains the deal that the young Matteo Alacran made with the governments of then-Mexico and the United States, which was that he'd stop the flow of "illegals" in exchange for land to grow drugs that he promised to "peddle only in Europe, Asia, and Africa" (168). Matt's heart "swells with pride" when he reads that his progenitor built a "vast empire stretching from central California all across Arizona and into New Mexico ... [and became] its supreme leader, dictator and führer" (168). He doesn't know what the word *führer* means, "but it was obviously something very good." Matt sees only the transformation from powerlessness to power, a shift that Matt hopes might one day be his own story. The book he's reading, which has been published by the Anti-Slavery Society of California, challenges Matt's view, describing El Patrón as an "evil, vicious, self-serving man." Matt throws the book down in a fury, thinking that the writer, a woman named Esperanza Mendoza, must simply be jealous. We see again the importance of becoming a good reader, of accepting—or at least listening to—narratives that might challenge our certainties. Matt's furious refusal of a counternarrative about El Patrón (about his own past, in essence) marks him as still in thrall to the monster who had him created. Like Maggie Hoskie—and anyone who would espouse a cosmopolitan perspective—Matt must develop what Anzaldúa describes as "a tolerance for contradictions, a tolerance for ambiguity" (101). Monsters thrive in the spaces where ambiguity and contradiction are erased.

The false consciousness that El Patrón is a rags-to-riches hero sustains Matt, just as the lost boys in the labor camp fantasize that they will be reunited with their parents and someday be released from the labor camp. The guards at the plankton factory tell the boys that if they work hard and "keep their records clear, they can move up to full citizenship when they reach eighteen" (*House of Scorpion* 279). The boys are never told what country will take them, and the working conditions are so terrible that most of them will die long before their eighteenth birthdays. The lie in this promise is revealed at the end of the second book, when Matt discovers that neither the United States nor Aztlán wants unskilled workers, who are "unpersons" in the eyes of both governments. Commodity culture wrecks lives and wrecks the planet—the consequence of searching for a "bargain." The boys are trapped in a system perpetuated by violence and falsehood; they are units of production, kept docile in part by aphorisms that would make Orwell proud: Individualism is like a five-legged horse, work is freedom and freedom is work. "In the new Aztlán, we don't have time for hobbies," a guard tells Matt. "We have to contribute to the general good of the people" (262). Given this emphasis on work and productivity, Matt thinks it makes sense that the workers should all be microchipped, as El Patrón has done to the workers in his fields, so that they can be made to work harder. His suggestion is greeted with outrage because to be chipped is to become a "zombie"—a monster—and the boys and the guards are "human."

The threat of becoming a monster—a zombie—also illustrates why the inhabitants of the plankton factory remain where they are: They are sure that they are less abject than the zombies, and if they escape they might be captured by the vampire king. As Braidotti points out in "Becoming-world", "governance by terror is one of the features of our historical condition and ... engenders a negative vision of pan-humanity ... as linking us all in shared vulnerability to viruses, environmental disasters and terrorist attacks by suicide and other kinds of bombers" (31). Fear of the monster becomes a tool that reinforces the categories and structures of an unjust society and enables that society to continue its destructive, extractive practices. The threat of monstrosity demarcates the boundaries of what is acceptable—a boundary that can also function as a prison.

Matt's time at the plankton factory and his experiences as a migrant give YA readers an opportunity to see how stereotypes are constructed: through manipulative narratives that produce fear and stasis (the way things are is the natural order) and through unjust laws that may have their roots in mercenary motives. As we become better readers of these narratives—less reliant on simple binaries—we become better able to "dismantle[e] the stereotypes that support group hatred," which is what philosopher Martha Nussbaum says about the power and utility of literature. Literature, Nussbaum says, enables us "to see the world, for a time, through [a character's] eyes and then reflect as spectators on the meaning of what we have seen" (92). We also see that good intentions alone are often not enough to dismantle stereotypes or challenge unjust systems. When Matt decides that an eejit called "Waitress" should be freed and renamed Marisol, for example, his actions result in Waitress and another eejit almost getting killed and Matt himself attacking an older man (also an eejit) who had been trying to teach Matt about how Opium works. Matt fails to "liberate" Waitress because he refuses to understand how the system works and he refuses to listen to anyone's advice. While his ultimate goal may have been good, his mode of achieving it was dictatorial and hierarchical.

Dismantling El Patrón's monstrous vision will require a deeper and more thorough realignment.

Monsters are entangled with questions of empire, which are in turn embedded in the dire circumstances of environmental damage. The devastation of the Gulf of California, which creates a whale graveyard in which Matt and Chacho almost die, marks the furthest boundary of Opium. The country itself is a patchwork of toxic fields and—surprisingly—a few isolated areas that are beginning to recover, a recovery that occurs almost entirely due to the fact that they are uninhabited and uncultivated. Flying in a hovercraft piloted by Cienfuegos, an eejit in charge of Opium's border guards, Matt and Listen, a young female clone who had been bred to serve as the replacement of another drug lord's long-dead wife, see the deserted towns and burned-out buildings that were abandoned when residents were forcibly removed to the United States or Aztlán when El Patrón came to power. It's a futuristic version of the destruction of indigenous communities in the Southwestern United States (and elsewhere), all in the service of capitalism.[7] "Thousands died," Cienfuegos tells Matt and Listen. Matt still wants to believe that El Patrón's plan for the creation of Opium was brilliant, but with every new encounter and conversation, he is forced to revise his opinions. He asks Cienfuegos to tell him if the plan to isolate Opium and only sell drugs outside Aztlán and the United States was a good idea, hoping for an unequivocal yes. Cienfuegos won't give him the satisfaction of an easy answer, saying only "in the long run, who can say" (169). The only reason Cienfuegos hesitates is because El Patrón unintentionally "preserved the ecosystem" not only by forcing humans to evacuate the area but also by constructing a force field around the country. The sky over Tucson is a brilliant blue instead of a polluted brown; the rivers bubble with clear water, the hills are green, and animals, including lions, roam the landscape, descendants of beasts that escaped from the Tucson Zoo. "Neglect is probably what preserved this place," says Cienfuegos, before flying them to another manifestation of ecological preservation: A miles-long biosphere, set in the northernmost territory of Opium. Lest Matt think that the biosphere was constructed out of some beneficent impulse by El Patrón, Cienfuegos tells him that the structure was intended as a prototype for the Scorpion Star, the satellite that controls all the various electronics in Opium, including the eejit microchips and the force field that serves as a wall around the entire country. It is another version of the megadam paradox: The monstrosity that El Patrón created—an empire run by slaves that produces addictive drugs—has also, in the lee of his attention, enabled the earth to renew itself.

The biosphere offers Matt multiple possibilities for what might be possible in the aftermath of El Patrón, including a way of thinking about "the good of the people" that is neither malicious nor illusory. Inside the biosphere are versions of all the world's ecosystems, from deserts to tundra to coastlines, as well as living quarters and a "fungus room." Inhabitants of the biosphere think that "Outside" is the stuff of legend, much the way that the boys in the plankton factory are sure that the land of Opium is "Dreamland." In both instances, the legends serve to keep people in their place: The boys stay at the factory and the biosphere residents stay inside because they are sure the Outside is so toxic it will kill them. Multiple generations live inside the habitat, and they are suspicious of Matt not because he is a clone but because he is, literally, an "outsider." When Cienfuegos introduces Matt as El Patrón to the first person they meet in the sphere—a frog-herder— the man says there's no way that Matt can be El Patrón. He's never heard of such a word and in fact rejects the entire category of "master," saying "no one owns nature. We are all Earth's creatures" (*Lord of Opium* 181). The frog-herder declares himself to be one of earth's creatures, even though the only "earth" he knows is the planet that exists inside the biosphere. He exists outside Opium's official narrative, which positions El Patrón as ruler and savior.

The biosphere exists outside the hierarchies with which Matt is familiar; it is a different, more humane, version of the plankton factory. Both places rely on a set of workers who cannot leave and both purport to be for the good of the people, but in the biosphere, the food is palatable (made from bugs and plants) and the aphorisms that people repeat aren't designed for abjection but connection: "We are all Gaia's creatures," the residents say before their communal meals. Children in the biosphere do no labor but are instead tended to in the "Brat enclosure," where they stay until they are fourteen. At fourteen, the children all enter a state of "dormancy," while "knowledge of the tasks they must perform as adults" is put into their brains. It is brainwashing of a sort, but unlike the microchipping of the eejits, this enforced knowledge does not erase agency. When Matt peeks into the Brat enclosure, he sees children who are "all perfect, with no deadness in their eyes. They were loved. They were wanted. They were happy" (*Lord of Opium* 194). These children are the opposite of the children in the plankton factory: Instead of being abandoned or orphaned, they have multiple parental figures; their value has nothing to do with their abilities as workers or as potential organ donors. Within the structure of the biosphere, the traditional family unit has been eradicated. Changing the definition of family parallels changing the relationship between humans and the planet. Just as no one "owns" the children, so too no one owns the planet. The well-being of the planet is a responsibility shared by everyone: It is that well-being that is truly "for the good of the people."

The mushrooms in the biosphere, which fascinate Cienfuegos, are (to make a bad pun) at the root of the possibilities offered by the novel. Like everything else in the biosphere, the mushrooms are the antithesis of what's in the outside world: Instead of the pollution created by the toxic drug fields, the mushrooms in fact detoxify their environment. The Mushroom Master shows them mushrooms that eat oil, pesticides, bacteria, even radioactive material.[8] Cienfuegos realizes that he and other agriculturists have made huge mistakes in their approach to cleaning the soil. Instead of thinking organically, they've only tried technological methods, developing ever more sophisticated pesticides and herbicides. Cienfuegos asks the Mushroom Master to take him on as a student—if Matt will give him permission. The microchipping won't allow Cienfuegos to do anything outside his programming without explicit permission from "the boss." The mushrooms illustrate the possibility that the earth can at least partially heal itself from human-created toxicity and provide a symbol of the readjustments needed to avert further environmental disaster. To recognize something as humble as the mushroom as key to ecological restoration—rather than humanity's "triumphs of engineering"—necessitates seeing the earth itself as a partner and teacher, rather than the literal ground on which humans present their mastery.

Matt can see the potential of the mushrooms, but he has a harder time accepting that Cienfuegos and the Mushroom Master are making decisions without him about how best to use the mushrooms in the Outside. The two men have developed a kind of fungi factory, telling

Matt that building the equipment "only cost us a ton or so of opium" and that they'd planned to alert Matt to what they were doing when they were "further along" (*Lord of Opium* 268). Their plan is to help the mycelia sprout faster and then use the spores to clean the highly toxic soil around the eejit pens. Cienfuegos presents the logic of the mushrooms in the framework of working for the greater good: "[W]hat use is the biosphere if we allow the rest of the world to die?" The voice of El Patrón that sits in Matt's head is not convinced: "[T]here is no 'us' involved here. Cienfuegos isn't the Lord of Opium" (287). Matt knows that if the old man were alive, he'd have killed both men for proceeding without his consent. But Matt also realizes that allowing Cienfuegos to proceed is another step toward dismantling Opium's destructive hierarchy.

In wrestling with his tyrannical inner voice, Matt wrestles not only with the creation of his own sense of self but also with how to think about freedom. El Patrón's ideas about freedom are similar to those expressed by The Hand in *Alif the Unseen*, which is that most people don't want actual freedom: "[P]eople want their governments to keep secrets from them. They want the hand of law to be brutal . . . . The world is returning to its natural state, to the rule of the weak by the strong" (267). That view of freedom is, in turn, a version of freedom that aligns with the CAs in *Parable of the Talents*, who are sure that theirs is the only narrative of truth. Listening to Cienfuegos and the Mushroom Master make plans, Matt realizes that "the country's problem [had been] that no one except the old man had been allowed freedom . . . [everyone] had been made part of a monstrous machine. A sterile machine feeding on the surplus bodies of the neighboring countries. There were no families or children. Left alone, it would die" (*Lord of Opium* 270). The clones and eejits and zombies are not the monsters, nor are they mythic demi-gods like Maggie or Kai. The monsters are those that see everything in terms of commodity—human, nonhuman, plant, animal, mineral. Matt's analogy connects the plankton factory, the factory of the biosphere, and the mushroom factory: three different ways of standardizing production, in a sense, and three ways of employing people within these factories. Of the three, the mushroom factory works the most organically with the planet because there is no dramatic intervention, only a gentle hastening of the sporing process. Cienfuegos and Mushroom Master

work with the mushrooms because they want to; they train anyone
who is interested. The process is volitional and reciprocal—they train
others to become Mushroom Masters even as they are learning from
the mycelia. The structure of the mycelium—a horizontal spreading
rather than a hierarchical scaffolding—might be a lesson for how to
reorganize the social structures of Opium.[9]

Matt had already had a lesson about the mutability of social structures when he discovered that, after the death of El Patrón, he is no
longer considered livestock. Toward the end of Book One, after Matt
escapes from the plankton factory and makes his way to the nunnery
where Maria goes to school. Maria's mother, Esperanza, tells him that
the law defining him as an "unperson" is nothing but a "wicked fiction [designed] to make it possible to use clones for transplants" by
stipulating that there cannot be two versions of the same person alive
at the same time. So as long as El Patrón is alive, Matt is an unperson,
and while Esperanza says she disapproves of the law, she makes sure
to send her daughter to school as far away from Matt as possible. She
doesn't want to risk her daughter being romantically involved with a
clone. In the aftermath of El Patrón's death, nothing about Matt has
changed, only the social structures that govern the disposition of his
previously monstrous body. The question of the monster is an abiding
social question: What do we do with inconvenient bodies? Do those in
power deem certain bodies to be monstrous so that they can be readily
disposed of, made expendable—an exploitable resource, like water or
arable soil?

Matt confronts Audre Lorde's still-relevant question about whether
the master's tools will ever dismantle the master's house: At the end
of the first novel, just after he comes to power, he vows to break El
Patrón's empire, free the eejits, rip up the drug crops, and create an
entirely new society. He has broken free of the narrative that situates El Patrón as a hero, but, as we see almost immediately in Book
Two, his optimism is wildly misplaced. The deeply entrenched systems
of El Patrón's empire have changed things so profoundly that simply
ripping them out would be as destructive as leaving them in place,
just as with the megadam in *Storm of Locusts*. Matt and those around
him must struggle with the same question that plagues Harry Potter
in *The Deathly Hallows*, and Lauren Olamina: How do we adjudicate
what to do "for the greater good"? And what do we do with all of

the destruction that has been wrought in the (supposed) service of the greater good?

Matt's nonhuman origins never change, but the stories that get told about those origins affect how he is understood by those around him and how he understands himself. As he learns to think differently about himself, outside the narratives laid down by El Patrón, he can enable changes in the structures of the society. It is as if Matt and others have learned what Merlin Sheldrake writes about in *Entangled Lives: How Fungi Make Our Worlds, Change Our Minds and Shape Our Futures* (2020): "I wanted to let these organisms lure me out of my well-worn patterns of thought, to imagine the possibilities they face, to let them press against the limits of my understanding, to give myself permission to be amazed—and confused—by their entangled lives" (29). Another possibility offered by the conclusion of Farmer's duology is the romance between Matt and Esperanza's daughter Maria, celebrated by a chaste kiss and Matt's proposal of marriage. The prospect of marriage raises questions: Can a cloned body produce offspring? If there are children, will they be considered clone–human hybrids, or will Matt's legal status prevail so that the children are seen only as human? The novels thus conclude not only with a vision of a healthier, less toxic planet, but also with the image of a monster that is loved, ultimately redefining our understanding of family.

Notes

1. Roanhorse has promised a third book in the "Sixth World" series, but no publication date has yet been announced.
2. Roanhorse admits that she is deliberately vague about Maggie's age, although it seems as if she's not even twenty.
3. According to the Indian Law Resource Center, "More than 4 in 5 American Indian and Alaska Native women have experienced violence, and more than 1 in 2 have experienced sexual violence" ("Ending Violence").
4. "Keshmish" is the Diné word for Christmas, but it refers to the time of year rather than any Christian faith-based tradition.
5. We might also think about the Ohmu, the huge bugs that inhabit the toxic landscape in Hayao Miyazaki's film *Nausicaä of the Valley of the Wind*. Seen as monstrous by almost everyone except Nausicaä, the Ohm are persecuted and threatened with destruction. Only after Nausicaä sacrifices herself in order to save a baby Ohm and is then reborn—the Christ metaphors are impossible to ignore—do the other inhabitants understand that the Ohm are not a threat, despite their nonhuman shape.

6. *Never Let Me Go*, Kazuo Ishiguro's novel about cloned children raised to be organ donors was published in 2005, three years after Farmer's novel.

7. See Nixon, *Slow Violence and the Environmentalism of the Poor*, for more real-world details about this destruction; also Alex Steffen, "The Transapocalyptic Now"; Todd Miller, *Storming the Wall: Climate Change, Migration, and Homeland Security* (2017), and many others.

8. Farmer adds a note in novel's paratextual material that says the Mushroom Master is based on Paul Stamets, who runs a business called Fungi Perfecti. Stamets (and others) say that mycelium can detoxify the soil. Stamets wrote an article in *Permaculture* suggesting how gomphidius mushrooms could help clean the soil around radioactive spills. Farmer's note suggests that she sees her story as an intervention in the ongoing arguments about how best to combat climate change, just as other notes in the paratextual material make clear that the novel wants to intervene in controversies over US–Mexico border policies.

9. Anna Lowenhaupt Tsing examines the literal and metaphorical possibilities of mushrooms in her book *The Mushroom at the End of the World: On the Possibility of Life in Capitalist Ruins* (2015).

3

Making Bridges

Early in *House of Scorpion*, Matt asks Celia if she has been microchipped, and she responds with such rage that she reminds Matt of "the Aztec goddess Coatlicue, who wore a necklace of severed hands" (*House of Scorpion* 35). Matt doesn't mean to insult Celia with his question; he'd only thought that, because she wasn't horrified by his status as a clone, perhaps she too was technologically modified. He doesn't know anything about Aztecs or their religion; he's only seen Coatlicue on television. And yet his comparison is accurate, when we consider it in conjunction with Gloria Anzaldúa's description of the ancient deity: Coatlicue balances "the dualities of male and female, light and dark, life and death" (*Borderlands/La Frontera* 54). Celia nurtures Matt while she slowly poisons him with arsenic, a lethal action intended to save his life: If Matt's organs are contaminated by arsenic, he becomes use-less to El Patrón as an organ donor, which means that Matt will live and El Patrón will die. Celia wields the power of life and death over her master through her ability to manipulate Matt's body and she has decided that El Patrón has lived too long. She tells him, "you've had your eight lives ... it's time to make your peace with God" (*House of Scorpion* 234).

The blur between Catholic and Aztec is just one of the many boundary-blurrings that happen in Farmer's novel, which seems in-debted to Anzaldúa's work. In *Borderlands/La Frontera* (1987), which launched the entire field of "border studies," Anzaldúa calls for a re-examination of the borderlands between the United States and Mexico and, in particular, a revision and reappropriation of the term *mestiza*, as a way to honor the multiplicity of identities that exist in the borderlands. Anzaldúa's book brings together multiple languages, genres, and experiences in order to lift up the borderlands as a site of power and resistance. Her work calls out the inadequacies and limitations of what Appiah calls "local allegiances." We cannot find allegiance with "the local" if that space is a site of repression or silencing, or if—as with El Patrón's entire estate—the entire localized space is nothing more than a fiefdom. The novel further interrogates ideas of the local through representations of religious practice, as with the altar dedicated to Guadalupe that Celia has in her bedroom. Anzaldúa describes Guadalupe as a "defender of the Mexican people" but reminds us that the saint's origins rest in Tonantsi, another "Azteca Mexican" female deity, "who gave Mexico the cactus plant to provide her people with milk and pulque" (50). Guadalupe is therefore a "synthesis of the old world and new ... a symbol of our rebellion against the rich, upper and middleclass; against the subjugation of the poor and *indio*" (52). It should not be surprising that in Farmer's novels, set as they are in the contested space of the border between Mexico and the United States, the borders between systems and ideologies are also contested, and frequently blurred into nonexistence.

Matt's story highlights the constraining power of local allegiances, which in his case confine him to the status of livestock. Appiah suggests that cosmopolitanism moves between the local and the global and that "loyalties and local allegiances determine more than what we want; they determine who we are [...] A creed that disdains the partialities of kinfolk and community may have a past, but it has no future" (*Cosmopolitanism* xviii). He also argues that our obligations to one another should not preclude anyone from "the right to go their own way" (xv), sounding for all the world like a cosmopolitan Fleetwood Mac. But what if the local is untenable for reasons of gender or sexuality or any other of a host of possibilities, and thus precludes people from "the right to go their own way"? Can we destabilize the boundaries of the local, reappropriate the space so that it becomes salutatory? Farmer's novel offers several examples of this reappropriation, as do the other novels that I discuss in this chapter.

Farmer uses the figure of Jesus Malverde, another product of the mixed and evolving culture of the borderlands, to reimagine local space, in a method similar to Anzaldúa's characterization of Guadalupe. Malverde is the name given to an early twentieth-century folklore hero who, while not himself a drug trafficker, is thought of as a "narco-saint,"[1] and is the patron saint for those who have been separated from their families. El Patrón—the cause of these separations—has all the statues of Malverde painted with his likeness as if to suggest that only through his intervention can anyone hope to be saved. Sor Artemesia, a nun from the Convent of Santa Clara in Aztlán who has joined Matt in Opium, does not think Malverde is a real saint, but she nonetheless tells Matt and the others that they must "honor the shreds of religion" of those who do believe in him. Artemesia prods Matt to "get off your butt and do the job God has given you," which in her mind means blowing up the Scorpion Star, the satellite that controls Opium's electronics. She tells Matt that killing the people aboard the satellite is a small price to pay in comparison to the "ten thousand or more buried under the fields" (*Lord of Opium* 338). The end, in her mind, justifies the means, and her logic helps Matt see his actions as different from those of El Patrón, who once blew up a commercial airliner that accidently flew into Opium's airspace. Blowing up the Scorpion Star may be violent, but like Luke Skywalker blowing up the Death Star in *Star Wars*, Matt's actions also save countless thousands from destruction and free the eejit slaves. The fact that Artemesia and Matt have the conversation about the Scorpion Star in the Malverde chapel suggests the final dismantling of El Patrón's empire: The chapel is no longer a site of homage but will become a space of sanctuary and refuge where the released eejits can rest before making their way home. The "shreds of religion" that Artemesia sees in Malverde and her insistence that freedom for many matters more than the lives of those who allied themselves with El Patrón offer another illustration of reappropriating the local so that it becomes a site of resistance rather than oppression.

As women of faith whose ability to nurture is tempered by a realistic apprehension that violence might sometimes be necessary, Celia and Artemesia can also be seen as examples of what Carol Breckenridge calls, in her critique of mainstream theories of cosmopolitanism, "cosmofeminism." Through the alliances they create—Celia with Matt, Artemesia with the eejits, each woman with the other—the two women create the space for Matt to reckon with, and ultimately renounce, the genetic legacy of El Patrón and remap the geographies of Opium. El Patrón never listened to women; he didn't think they were worth his time. The simple fact that Matt heeds the advice given by Celia and Artemesia is itself a realignment of El Patrón's tyrannical local systems. These local systems shift into what Breckenridge describes as "spheres of intimacy," which are similar to Haraway's non-natal kinship groups or what I've called here "affiliative communities." Regardless of nomenclature, these groups bring pressure on local allegiances in ways that not only loosen local strictures but also enable a more capacious sense of global or extra-local connection.

Almost as if she anticipates Appiah's invocation of the local, Anzaldúa demonstrates the need to be more critical of it by brushing away the conventional (patriarchal, racist, heteronormative) understandings of *mestizaje* specifically and the borderlands more generally. In their introduction to the fourth edition of *Borderlands/La Frontera*, Norma Élia Cantú and Aída Hurtado point out that Anzaldúa's writings have sparked generations of conversation and modes of resistance that enable "social action and coalition building," which are, in turn, achieved through "self-reflexivity and seeing through the 'eyes of others' ... to gain a deeper understanding than can be achieved by staying within one's social milieu" (8). Anzaldúa herself, writing in the introduction to the first edition in 1987, talks about learning to see herself anew, as if she is swimming "in a new element" that is awakening "dormant areas of consciousness" (*Borderlands/La Frontera* np). *Borderlands/La Frontera* reinvents the local, finds power in what had been an abjected identity. We might even say that the book is a speculative fiction that draws on local knowledge to carve out new modes of resistance to the erasing impulse of dominant culture.

Anzaldúa's writings show how "the local" can become a source of resistance, in part because, as we see with El Patrón and the Malverde chapel, dominant powers cannot easily coopt individual (or communal) imagination or belief. This realignment of the local can be seen in terms of what Raymond Williams talks about in his classic study, *Marxism and Literature* (1977). In this book Williams maps out the relationships between what he calls dominant, residual, and emergent cultures in order to explain how dominant cultures fail to subsume all aspects of a society. What dominant cultures exclude, he says, "may often be seen as the personal or the private, or as the natural or even the metaphysical. Indeed it is usually in one or the other of these terms that the excluded area is expressed, since what the dominant has effective seized is the ruling definition of the social" (125). The dominant culture may be able to define what it means as "society," and try to dictate the realities of those societies, but the intangibles of faith and feeling are much more difficult to structure. Celia and Sor Artemesia use precisely those qualities that El Patrón disdains—compassion and religion—to create spheres of intimacy that resist and ultimately dismantle his systems. At the end of the novel, Matt has implemented a nonhierarchical set of systems and helped establish affiliative communities that offer refuge to the eejits who have been "depersoned" by their countries and to the orphaned children who have nowhere else to go.

Haraway points out that all too often fears about "non-natalist" modes of kinship are fueled by fears about immigrants and fantasies of "racial purity." She asks what would happen if we looked for "non-natalist innovation … in queer, decolonial, and indigenous worlds instead of to European, EuroAmerican, Chinese, or Indian rich and wealth-extracting sectors" ("Anthropocene, Capitalocene" 163). The "Brat enclosure" in Opium's biosphere might be one such example; we could also look to the collective child-caring that happens in *Parable of the Sower* as the travelers walk north or to the jinn-human baby in *Alif the Unseen*, who will be tended to by a loose confederation of magical and non-magical beings. Haraway's vision of non-natalist kinship groups is not new—"it takes a village," as the saying goes—but definitions of family that challenge two-parent heteronormativity are still seen as somehow exceptional and, in the United States at least, somehow destabilizing to the state of the State.[2] Because caring for others—particularly children, the elderly, the infirm or unwell—is at the heart of kinship groups, those groups can also, by extension, suggest models for larger communities, even nations. As communities form, locally and domestically, so too do larger structures, and a nonhierarchical kinship group, rooted in a redefined and more capacious sense of "local," could spread, mycelium-like, in ways that make national borders irrelevant and immaterial. We see, therefore, the links between emergent practices—particularly those rooted in religious traditions—and the shift of emphasis away from national or State-based identities to non-natal kinship groups as a source of power, resistance, and safety.

Farmer's novels are an example of reimagining the local as a challenge to dominant, environmentally destructive systems, as does Nalo Hopkinson's *Brown Girl in the Ring* (1998), set in a futuristic dystopian Toronto, and Nnedi Okorafor's "Nsibidi Scripts" trilogy: *Akata Witch* (2011), *Akata Warrior* (2017), and *Akata Woman* (2022), all set in contemporary Nigeria. In these novels, emergent practices based on spiritual traditions fuel resistance to dominant cultures and foster non-natal kinship groups that help realign local allegiances. Ti-Jeanne, the young teenage mother at the center of *Brown Girl in the Ring*, and Sunny Azuwe, the protagonist of the *Akata* books, who is twelve in the first book and sixteen in the third, exist in worlds that highlight what it means to live "post-nation." National identity seems irrelevant as a marker; identity is forged instead through communities that eschew a capitalist ethos in favor of prioritizing the health of the planet. To create these communities, Hopkinson and Okorafor turn to old stories and spiritual practices—from the Caribbean and West Indies for Hopkinson, and from Nigeria for Okorafor. In the context of the novels, these old stories find new directions, and in that shifting, the dominant culture is itself challenged. As Okorafor says, readers are always surprised by how much she doesn't have to make up: What looks "fantastic" from one perspective is, from another, a deeply held belief that some say should not be challenged. In a 2017 interview with *The New York Times*, Okorafor commented on the reaction to *Akata Witch* by religious conservatives in Nigeria: "They can read *Harry Potter* and be fine with it, but *Akata Witch* is evil" (Alter np). The local, in other words, makes *Akata Witch* something to avoid: Local allegiances can help us to read more carefully . . . or shut down reading altogether.

Both Sunny and Ti-Jeanne must grapple with realities of spiritual worlds about which they are initially skeptical and afraid. They both become adept practitioners within these realities, Sunny as a "Leopard" (the magical world into which she is initiated) and Ti-Jeanne as a seer and healer, and both are thrust into confrontations with destructive, malignant forces. The evil in their worlds is explicitly linked to the destructive power of a dominant society that privileges profit over everything else: The monsters of commodification and exploitation are what must be defeated. The powers that each girl possesses are derived from ancient beliefs that ultimately serve as modes of resistance to the Anglo-European legacies of colonialism and imperialism that have done such damage to the planet and its inhabitants.

In their merging of old ways and new, traditional practices and modern behaviors, these novels might also be characterized as

"Afrofuturist," which, like the term "emergent," helps us to conceptualize the practice of using what the dominant culture excludes precisely to challenge that dominance. A term coined by Mark Dery in 2008, "Afrofuturism" denotes "speculative fiction that treats African American themes and addresses African American concerns in the context of twentieth-century technoculture" (qtd. in Egbunike 142). Afrofuturism interrogates conventions and generates conversations, and in its willingness to engage with difference (of subject, of media, of style) it suggests a cosmopolitan ethos that decenters (or altogether bypasses) Western certainties. In Afrofuturism, arrayed against the individualist ethos of Western-style capitalism are ideas like compassion, fluidity, self-love without narcissism, and cosmopolitanism. The irreverence inherent in Afrofuturist performance—think George Clinton and Funkadelic, Sun-Rah, Erykah Badu—runs through these novels, reminding us that self-importance is not a virtue that enables community strength. Afrofuturism connotes the ability to reflect on one's culture with ironic distance, which Bryan Turner sees as an essential component of cosmopolitanism: "[I]rony and reflexivity produce a humanistic skepticism towards the grand narratives of modern ideologies" (57). Cosmopolitan irony "recognizes that our modern dilemmas cannot be solved simply by a naïve return to origins" (57). This irony does not mean that one cannot love one's country, but it does mean that any love of country must be tempered by distance and reflection.

Drawing on a playful mixing of sources and media, Afrofuturism creates speculative futures and challenges dominant ideologies. Hopkinson describes these challenges in her introduction to *So Long Been Dreaming* (2004), an anthology of postcolonial science fiction and fantasy: When people of color work in these genres, they "take on the meme of colonizing the natives and from the experience of the colonizee [sic], critique it, pervert it, fuck with it, with irony, with anger, with humor and also, with love and respect for the genre of science fiction that makes it possible to think about new ways of doing things" (8). These "new ways" are the emergent practices that push forward toward a more flexible and capacious present and thus create a sense of the local that is more hospitable to engagement with difference.

The YA novels of Okorafor and Hopkinson focus on nonwhite and non-Western perspectives, drawing connections between disparate, but frequently marginalized, traditions. Ti-Jeanne's grandmother says that she could be called a "myalist, bush doctor, iyorisha, curandera, four-eye, even obeah woman for them who don't understand [those other words]" (*Brown Girl* 218). Sunny's mentor Sugar Cream is a tiny woman with terrible scoliosis, who can shape-shift, talk to spiders, and who might be "Igbo, Haisa, Yoruba, Ijaw, Fulani, or another ethnicity" (*Warrior* 92) Origins and purity are irrelevant: What matters, as Mami tells Ti-Jeanne, is that you "love spirit," which is to say, that you look beyond yourself at the world to see how you might be of service. One aspect of loving spirit has to do with challenging limited and limiting narratives about what is possible, or even what is real. In their attitudes toward local cultures and traditions, these books embody an Afrofuturist ethos, which Ebony Elizabeth Thomas, in *The Dark Fantastic*, describes as "an aesthetic and an activist movement" that draws on speculative fiction, futurism, and "African diaspora culture" (9). As both activism and aesthetic, Afrofuturism implies a dynamic process of exploration and reanimation, reframing aspects of the local, including religious and iconographic traditions, while also challenging aspects of the local that may be limiting, oppressive, or static. Appiah sees a similar dynamism at work in the seemingly paradoxical quality of cosmopolitan patriotism, which involves "migration, nomadism, diaspora. In the past, these processes have too often been the result of forces we should deplore; the old migrants were often refugees, and older diasporas often began in an involuntary exile. But what can be hateful, if coerced, can be celebrated when it flows from the free decisions of individuals or of groups" ("Cosmopolitan Patriots" 618). The question of who gets to make those "free decisions" is key, and, as we will see in this chapter, the consequences of those decisions often result in expanding ideas of the local and reconfiguring a relationship not only to the community but to the planet.

Section One: *Brown Girl in the Ring*

In a 2008 interview, Nalo Hopkinson echoed Anzaldúa's ideas about the power of reshaping dominant culture: "My work comes from a Caribbean context," Hopkinson explains.

> Fusion fits very well; that's how we survived. We can't worship Shango on pain of death? Well, whaddya know; he just became

conflated with a Catholic saint. Got at least four languages operating on this one tiny island? Well, we'll just combine the four
and call it Papiamento. Can't grow apples in the tropics for
that apple pie? There's this vegetable called chocho, and it's
approximately the right color and texture and pretty tasteless;
add enough cinnamon, brown sugar, and nutmeg, and no one
will know the difference. It's a sensibility that I'm quite familiar
with and enamored of (and it's great for writing postapocalyptic
cities).

(Nelson 99)

In her first novel, *Brown Girl in the Ring*, Hopkinson uses this fusion
sensibility to create a post-apocalyptic vision of Toronto, most of which
has fallen into the "muddy water" of Lake Ontario, leaving behind an
area known as The Burn that is governed by a drug lord named Rudy,
who has—like Okoto/Black Hat, the villain in *Akata Witch*—mastered
traditional magic that he uses solely for his own gain.

Like the other speculative fiction that I discuss in this book, *Brown
Girl* reminds us about the power and necessity of being a good reader,
about the strength of affiliative communities, and about the need to
shift the boundaries of the local in order to find a more capacious
set of local allegiances that engage specificity without creating repression. The two intertwined stories of the novel center around Ti-Jeanne
and her grandmother, Mami (also known as Gros-Jeanne), who live
in The Burn and have been abandoned by Ti-Jeanne's mother, Mi-
Jeanne.[3] Ti-Jeanne, who is in her mid-teens, has a new baby, whose
father is a handsome ne'er-do-well in thrall to Rudy, who controls
The Burn. Rudy sells buff, an addictive narcotic made from poisonous
toads, but he also has a brisk sideline selling human organs, which he
harvests from the most vulnerable inhabitants of The Burn. Rudy co-
erces Tony, Ti-Jeanne's lover and a former nurse, into killing Mami
so that Rudy can sell her heart to the Canadian prime minister, who
needs a heart transplant. To avenge her grandmother's death and rid
The Burn of Rudy's tyranny, Ti-Jeanne must overcome her hostility
toward the world of the orishas, a world that Mami understands and
uses as a tool to minister to the community of The Burn.

At the beginning of the novel, Ti-Jeanne thinks she knows all that
she needs to know; her certainty is rooted in the pragmatics of daily

life, and she tells herself she has no need for Mami's spirits or anything else. When she delivers Mami's homemade remedies to a man who calls himself the librarian, she is uninterested in the display he's made about how Toronto fell apart. The city's environmental apocalypse began with the casual racism of capitalism and exploitation of natural resources: The Temagami tribe takes Ontario to court over land rights, and in retaliation the Canadian government cuts services to the province by 30%. As a result, the jobless rate rises, more services are cut, and then the "Government abandon[s] the city core" (*Brown Girl* 4). The Temagami tribe eventually wins its suit, but by that point, the satellite suburbs around Toronto have "raised roadblocks" to prevent the desperate city dwellers from entering their communities. The only "unguarded exit from the city core [is] . . . over water, by boat or prop plane," and the only people who remain are "the ones who couldn't or wouldn't leave. The street people. The poor people . . . [o]r [those] who saw the decline of authority as an opportunity" (4). Like Matt in *The House of Scorpion* when he first learns about El Patrón's history and wants to interpret it in whatever way is most convenient for him, Ti-Jeanne doesn't want to think about the complexities of the history or the legacy of exploitation that it illustrates. Instead she thinks, "all of that was old-time story. Who cared any more?"(*Brown Girl* 4). She cares only about what's in front of her; she refuses to see how her present moment is shaped by these past actions.

Her flippant comment will come back to haunt her, because it is her refusal to grapple with her own history—her specific traditions and local knowledge—that almost kills her. Ti-Jeanne doesn't believe Mami's old ways are particularly useful. She gives Mami's "nasty-smelling paste" to the librarian for his eczema but also passes along "vitamin B tablets and anti-inflammatory cream" that she'd found stashed away. She wants nothing to do with the spirit world, even to the point where she refuses to tell Mami about the visions she has of other people's deaths and of being visited by the "Jab-Jab," a West Caribbean spirit who is both threatening and benevolent (he protects Ti-Jeanne's baby from a malevolent spirit, for example). Jab-Jab is also Papa Legbara, "an Eshu, one of the guardians of the crossroads" (95). Ti-Jeanne "don't want to know nothing 'bout obeah, oui" (47), hoping that if she ignores the visions, they will go away. Mami warns her that ignoring the spirits is "stupidness," and that the consequences will be dire: "[I]f you don't learn how to use [the vision power], it will use you, just like it take your mother" (47). Ti-Jeanne's mother fled rather than grapple with her spiritual power; Ti-Jeanne must heed Mami's warnings and instructions or suffer the same fate.

Whether she likes it or not, Ti-Jeanne is already part of the spirit world, or rather, the spirit world is already a part of her: Papa Legbara is her "spirit father," a trickster figure that can help her defeat Rudy and avenge Mami's death, if she can learn how to listen to him. An unwed teenage mother makes an unlikely heroine for a fantasy novel, especially one who thinks of her baby as a "boulderstone that someone had given her to hold" (141). And yet it is this unconventional heroine who drives the plot of the novel, undoing our expectations of what "fantasy" might look like and offering us a way to reimagine the power of local knowledge as a means of resistance to dominant structures that want to silence or eradicate difference, challenge, questions.

The novel's swirl of cultures, traditions, and forms illustrates Hopkinson's idea that "for people from diasporic cultures there's more than a doubled consciousness. It's occupying multiple overlapping identities simultaneously . . . find[ing] modes of expression that convey how we've had to become polyglot, not only in multiple lexicons but also in multiple identities" (Rutledge 599). Mami explains her powers to Ti-Jeanne in this polyglot way: Her obeah is a version of "African powers, child. The spirits. The loas. The orishas. The oldest ancestors. You will hear people from Haiti and Cuba and Brazil and so call them different names [but] we all doing the same thing. Serving the spirits" (*Brown Girl* 126). The name or origin of the practice doesn't matter; what matters is "serving the spirits." Mami's words also explain why, when she is first trying to teach Ti-Jeanne about her visions, she reaches for a tarot deck that was given to her by "Romni [sic] Jenny." The Romany woman paints the Caribbean healer a set of tarot cards, joining their shared abilities for prophecy. They work in partnership, collaborating and strengthening their individual local traditions and, at the same time, creating a space for readers to connect their own beliefs and traditions to the action of the novel, regardless of where those beliefs originated.

This mixing continues in the people who come to Mami's obeah rituals, which she conducts in the ruins of what had been the Toronto

Crematorium Chapel and Necropolis. Ti-Jeanne hears "Caribbean English ... Spanish ... African-rhythmed French ... one or two [people] were White and there was Mami's friend Jenny, who was Romany" (87). The people left behind by the collapse of the government create their own community and are sustained by Mami's preaching, a positive aspect of Mami's spiritual practice that Ti-Jeanne refuses to acknowledge. The inhabitants of The Burn are a mixed bunch—people with names like Pavel, Roopsingh, Bruk-foot Sam, Frank Greyeyes—the immigrants and paupers who were left behind by the collapse of the government. Mami finds opportunity in this mixing, telling Ti-Jeanne that "Romni Jenny and Frank Greyeyes were teaching her about northern herbs" that she can use as substitutes for the Caribbean plants that do not grow in Canada. Mami's adaptability illustrates the ways in which "the local" can become a means of resistance: The old practices are reanimated in this new context. Her remedies and rituals help keep the community alive, physically and spiritually, and in a brutal irony, she will also become the impetus of a shift in the (white) government's attitude toward The Burn when her heart is transplanted into the body of the Canadian premier. Unlike Ti-Jeanne, Mami is comfortable with a porous boundary between the spirit world and her own. In her willingness to accept the irrational and unexpected, Mami is a much better reader than her granddaughter. She has accepted a paradoxical strategy for existence that Hopkinson espouses more broadly: "[T]he irrational, the inexplicable and the mysterious exist side by side each with the daily events of life. Questioning the irrational overmuch is unlikely to yield a rational answer, and may prove dangerous. Best instead to find ways to incorporate both the logical and the illogical into one's approach to the world" (Johnston 201). To defeat Rudy, Ti-Jeanne will need to learn this same lesson, in effect changing her perceptions about her local context by changing her structures of feeling.

Ti-Jeanne's ability to redefine her local allegiances comes to the fore when she is forced to hide from Rudy in a deserted underground mall, where she, Tony, and Baby have sought refuge with The Burn's abandoned street children. The children are the marginalized of the marginalized, homeless and vulnerable, often hunted by Rudy so that he can harvest their organs. They help Ti-Jeanne and her companions escape from Rudy's minions as a way of repaying their debt to Mami, who healed them when they got hurt. One of the teenagers in the group has been shot, and although Ti-Jeanne tries to help him, he dies in the arms of another young man, who "kissed his forehead with the tenderness of a lover" (*Brown Girl* 193). The group of children—queer, diasporic, dispossessed—agree to watch Baby while Ti-Jeanne tries to summon Legbara for help, using Mami's rituals without Mami's coaching. When Mami performs this summoning, the patterns she draws on the ground are "intricate," and the gifts she arrays for the spirits are precious: rum, chicken blood, cornmeal, tobacco. All Ti-Jeanne can find is a stale cigarette, two pieces of candy "dotted with pocket lint" (194), and a few smears of blood from Chu, lying dead in his lover's arms. Mami had tapped the ground in a complicated pattern, but Ti-Jeanne "doesn't dare beat out a rhythm with her fingers, for fear it would be the wrong one. All she could do was call on Legbara, her own personal Eshu" (195). Pushed to the margins by Rudy's quest for power, Ti-Jeanne reaches to the old ways as a source of power. And when her makeshift ritual does in fact summon Legbara, we see how these reconfigured traditions can be used as means of resistance. The faith, not the form, is what matters.

Legbara does not do the work of resistance himself, but communing with him gives Ti-Jeanne ideas about how to bypass Rudy's brute strength and powerful magic. Rudy is the opposite of Mami, Legbara says, in that he "make the spirit serve *he*" (219, italics in original). With magic that he learned from Mami, Rudy turns people into zombies and has imprisoned a "duppy spirit" in a large calabash, feeding it on human blood and using it as a kind of ghostly assassin. He sends the duppy after anyone who has displeased him, and although the duppy pleads to be free of its prison, Rudy refuses to relinquish that power. The duppy spirit also keeps Rudy preternaturally young; he is like El Patrón or Dorian Gray, feeding off those around him to satiate his own vanity. Rudy captures Ti-Jeanne and tortures her, explaining that eventually he will enslave her spirit and turn her into his new duppy. Legbara can't free Ti-Jeanne, but he reminds her of something that Mami had said before she was killed and that Ti-Jeanne hadn't understood at the time: that "the centre pole [is] the bridge between two worlds" (221). Terrified and seemingly helpless, trapped in Rudy's office on the top floor of the CN Tower, Ti-Jeanne suddenly understands: "[L]ike the spirit tree that the centre pole symbolized, the

CN Tower dug roots deep into the ground where the dead lived and pushed high into the heavens where the oldest ancestors lived" (221). Drawing on her own spiritual power, Ti-Jeanne makes herself the bridge that will allow the spirits to cross over and defeat Rudy.

Attempting to dominate, as Rudy does, leads to destruction, while a willingness to serve, as Mami did, strengthens the community. The bridge that Ti-Jeanne creates links the dead and the living, ancestors and contemporaries, history and future. In so doing, she rids The Burn of the tyrant who has preyed on the entire community. She calls on "every one Rudy kill to feed he duppy bowl ... climb the pole, al-lyou; climb the pole" (221) to extract their revenge. The ghosts of dead children mingle with the Ancestors to torment Rudy and kill his henchmen. Other Ancestors heal the wounds Rudy has inflicted on Ti-Jeanne and tell her that they know "she not going forget is who blood she come from" (226). Ti-Jeanne understands now what it means to be a seer-woman, and she has learned how to adapt these ancient practices to her contemporary moment. In so doing, she has freed the community from Rudy's tyranny.

By allowing herself to be the bridge between worlds, Ti-Jeanne has proven herself to be a powerful obeah practitioner, but that skill comes with danger, as Legbara tells her: "You do a thing I never see nobody do before.... you hold eight of the Oldest Ones in your head one time ... Don't try it again, eh? It could burn your brain out" (229). Mastery brings power but not comfort, even though Ti-Jeanne is re-lieved that Rudy and his henchmen have been destroyed. Comfort arrives in the form of the community, who offer her gifts of food as she walks through the market square after she defeats Rudy. The peo-ple of The Burn share her sense of loss about Mami's death, and in that communal feeling, Ti-Jeanne finds solace: "[G]rief still darkened her thoughts, but the attentions of the market people had soothed her a little" (232). In learning how to wield—and adapt—Mami's skills, Ti-Jeanne also learns about the power of belonging to a community.

Ti-Jeanne's final lesson comes in admitting her shortcomings and thus finding a connection to her mother, who abandoned her when she was a baby. Mi-Jeanne confesses that when Ti-Jeanne was born, motherhood seemed to "eat up my whole life. It was baby need this, baby need that. I couldn't take it. I sorry to admit it to you, Ti-Jeanne, but I couldn't take it" (242). Her comments hit Ti-Jeanne hard;

she feels "shame . . . a bit too close to the bone." The shame comes from realizing that "she knew what her mother had been feeling," because she too felt nothing but resentment and anger toward her own child (242). Ti-Jeanne recognizes the mistake of her harsh judgments and forgives both her mother and herself for feeling overwhelmed by the difficulties of new motherhood. Ti-Jeanne's spiritual mastery, in other words, is tempered by a sense of humility; she can be an adept without having to insist on certainty or control.

Compassion leads Ti-Jeanne to forgive her mother, but she will not forgive Tony for murdering Mami, which not only betrayed the love he claimed to have for Ti-Jeanne but also reduced Mami to nothing more than meat, a commodity. Ti-Jeanne allows Tony to join the communal celebration of Mami's passing, but realizes that she feels nothing for him: "[H]er heart [is] free." Her obsessive desire has vanished and all she feels for him is pity, as if he were one of the many patients that had been knocking on the door of her house asking for help. The steady stream of ailing community members have been sent by Legbara, as if to remind her of the power of Mami's legacy. Empowered by her own skills as a seer, Ti-Jeanne calls him out on his actions: "I go do this [tend the sick] for a little while, but I ain't Mami. I ain't know what I want to do with myself yet, but I can't be she" (245). She has learned to read the spirit world and made peace with her own mistakes, which will enable her to create her own local allegiances; she needn't follow in the path of anyone else.

The final twist in the novel rests in what happens to Mami's heart after it is transplanted into the body of Margaret Uttley, the prime minister. The merging of the two bodies becomes a medical version of Rudy's duppy. The heart that Rudy sells to Uttley's adviser is medically necessary, but the fact that it's a *human* heart is a political expediency: In the world of the novel, it would have been normal to use a pig heart, but Uttley's senior adviser tells her that her constituents are against "porcine organ farms" because of a "disease that had jumped from pigs to humans" (39). The adviser suggests that she should request a human heart, which they can present as "the safe, moral way to go: People Helping People, we'll call it" (40). When this plan is announced, support for Uttley grows among voters—except there is no available heart. Rudy's black-market organs are the only recourse. In her discussion of Hopkinson's novel, Rachel Stein points out that

Rudy's organ harvesting can be seen as "an ultimate form of biopiracy and bodily colonization that literally dismembers the colonized person in order to incorporate their body parts into the colonizer's body" (Stein 218). The fact that Mami's heart cures the leader of the government that abandoned her community becomes a key facet of the novel's political commentary.

Rudy controls the living through his manipulation of the dead, but Mami has the last laugh because her heart comes to control the body of the prime minister, physically and spiritually. A few days after the transplant, Uttley feels herself "losing the ability to control her own body" (*Brown Girl* 237). She blacks out, and when she regains consciousness, "the heart—her heart—was dancing joyfully between her ribs . . . she had worried for nothing. She was healed, a new woman now" (237). Readers figure out what happened when Uttley tells herself that her fears were "stupidness"—a word that only Mami uses. Uttley has become Mami's duppy, in a sense, although unlike Rudy's duppy, this one will "serve spirit" instead of the other way around. Mami/Uttley tells her advisers that she has a more humane plan to solicit organ donors and also that she wants to "rejuvenate Toronto . . . [by] offer[ing] interest-free loans to small enterprises" (240). The advisers protest, saying that the place is a "rat hole" and asking if Uttley has suddenly developed a "social conscience." Post-transplant Uttley embodies Mami's concern for the community and her ability to work across difference. Critics have debated how to read this section of the novel, pointing out that even if The Burn is revitalized, Ti-Jeanne is still without a grandmother. Others have suggested that we see the transplant scene as a metaphor of white Canada being saved by its diasporic residents. The multiple interpretations remind us that there are no easy solutions to our contemporary problems—not climate change, rapacious capitalism, or xenophobia. There may be gains, but there will also always be losses as we try to realign our local allegiances.

The creole spoken by many characters in the novel (except Uttley, significantly) reflect another aspect of the emergent path the novel carves for itself. Hopkinson points out that in the Caribbean, language has been "a tool of resistance and politicization . . . we have hybridized the different languages that were in operation in the Caribbean into creoles." Rather than see this representation of language as some kind of internalized racism or self-hatred because it veers away from "standard" English, she asks how else to convey the "the callaloo that is the Caribbean, that gives me a clan tartan, one Jewish great grandmother, and one Maroon, as well as Aboriginal, West African, and South Asian ancestry?" (Rutledge 600). Language becomes another facet of changing the white world of speculative and science fiction so that it becomes a site of greater possibility—a more capacious story. Robin Kimmerer, the Potawatomi ethnobotanist and essayist, talks about the efforts made at the turn of the twentieth century at places like the Carlisle Indian school in Pennsylvania, where her grandfather was sent, to erase Native languages. Potawatomi, the language her grandfather spoke, "is an affront to the ears of the colonist in every way, because it is a language that challenges the fundamental tenets of Western thinking—that humans alone are possessed of rights and all the rest of the living world exists for human use" ("Speaking of Nature"). She goes on to point out what theorists like Edward Said have long observed, which is that "linguistic imperialism has always been a tool of colonization, meant to obliterate history and the visibility of the people who were displaced along with their languages" (Kimmerer, "Speaking of Nature"). Creole becomes another way for Hopkinson to write back against empire; Mami's Creole voice comes out of Uttley's mouth: She tells her adviser, "don't get your panties in a twist, man. Stupidness" (*Brown Girl* 239). Hopkinson says that science and speculative fiction have "always been subversive . . . used to critique social systems . . . and that's when I find [it] compelling" (Rutledge 591). The layers of critique in the novel bridge history and present, imperialism and environmentalism; we are asked to consider the power of "serving spirit" as a means of powerful resistance, even as we are asked to reimagine our ideas of what a YA hero might look like: a teenage mother with a bad attitude and a strong community spirit.

Section Two: Nsibidi Scripts

Sunny Nwazue confuses people: "I am American and Igbo, Nigerian by blood, American by birth, and Nigerian again because I live there. I have West African features . . . but while the rest of the family is dark brown, I have light yellow hair, skin the color of 'sour milk,' . . . and hazel eyes that look like God ran out of the right color. I'm albino"

(*Witch* 3). The confusion only increases when she discovers that she is part of a magic race called "the Leopard People": Leopards think she is a genetic anomaly—a "free agent"—because she is a Leopard whose parents are both "Lambs," which is what Leopards call non-magical humans. Sunny, like Ti-Jeanne, must learn how to bridge the disparate realities in which she lives, a challenge made more difficult for Sunny because she does not grow up with these various worlds but instead stumbles into her own power, oblivious to the ramifications.

Sunny is the only person in her family who was born in the United States; she is Igbo because her parents are, but she speaks the language with an American accent that her classmates in Aba find laughable, just as her American classmates mocked her Nigerian intonations. She feels more at home with the Leopards than she does with her Lamb family, particularly her patriarchal father. The Leopards provide a space where Sunny feels most herself, albeit with some trepidation: In the Leopard world, she exists alongside powerful spiders, art-making wasps, and malevolent river spirits. As an albino, Sunny seems strange in both worlds, but as a Leopard, her albinism gives her the gift of easily becoming invisible, a skill that others find incredibly difficult. Over the course of the trilogy, Sunny begins to see how her power and the power of her friends can be utilized against evil, embodied as the pervasive destruction created by Western oil companies. The locals—both Leopard and Lamb—who enable the oil companies are represented as having put individual profit ahead of community and planetary health.

The Leopard People with whom Sunny feels a sense of kin are based on the Ekpe, a secret society that flourished primarily in West Africa and that, while still extant, now fulfills a mostly ceremonial role. In her essay about *Akata Witch*, Louisa Uchum Egbunike points out that the Ekpe were "multicultural and transnational" and that, by drawing on the organization as the basis for the Leopard People (*ekpe* means leopard), Okorafor's novel suggests that "Africa holds the solutions to its own problems" (149). The Ekpe had four major roles in precolonial life, including community policing, providing community entertainments and the conferral of citizenship within the Ekpe, as well as the provision of a "school for esoteric teachings regarding the human life as a cyclic process of regeneration, with the eventual reincarnation of that being" (Egbunike 149). Leopard magic may be rooted in local and precolonial tradition, but what marks a Leopard adept is the ability to evolve, to engage with the contemporary world in capacious, multiple ways. So, for instance, when the giant spider Udide, in *Akata Warrior*, conjures a magical creature called a "grasscutter"—a kind of flying buffalo—the creature is soothed by listening to hip-hop. Grashcoatah, as it calls itself, is partial to Nas's *Hip Hop is Dead* and to the singing of Jill Scott. Once Grashcoatah is listening to music, Sunny's friend Sasha can "ask him what we [need] to ask him . . . [and] he's cool with it" (*Warrior* 374). The magical creature from legend mollified by contemporary music becomes an illustration of "new forms or adaptations of form" that lead to powerful modes of resistance. Provided Grashcoatah is happy, Sunny and her friends can fly to a magical kingdom unreachable by other methods and attempt to destroy Ekwensu, the evil spirit that threatens not only Nigeria but also the environmental health of the planet.

Ekwensu is the evil spirit in the *Akata* novels, a figure from Nigerian folklore whose destructive powers are expressed in the form of environmental destruction. Linking the ancient spirit with the contemporary crisis, in the form of oil spills, fires, and drought, brings together centuries of Anglo-European exploitation of Nigerian resources. In *Akata Witch*, Ekwensu has been newly summoned by Black Hat, a Leopard also known as Okoto, who studied Leopard magic with Sunny's grandmother, then killed her and went on to "do big business with [the] United States of America [that made him] economically wealthy enough to push his plan forward" (18). Okoto mixes Leopard magic with American capitalism; he is responsible not only for the death of children (the "Black Hat murders" terrorize the Lamb world) but also the death of the environment.[4] The final battle in *Akata Witch* takes place at a gas station, where Sunny's spirit face, called Anyanwu, fights Ekwensu: Two Nigerian spirits fighting at a gas station, a symbol of Western exploitation of a Nigerian resource. Defeated by Anyanwu, Ekwensu slowly vanishes into the mud, reminding Sunny of "the Wicked Witch of the West's death in *The Wizard of Oz*. Ekwensu wasn't melting, but she looked like she was" (*Witch* 327). Sunny's reference to the Hollywood story about the importance of home does not suggest the power of US cultural imperialism but rather the opposite: the separation of US cultural referents from cultural hegemony. Brian T. Edwards suggests that this detachment is one aspect of living "after the American century." In this era, he argues, the American "cultural product—and sometimes more importantly the form it takes—detaches from the source culture ... US hegemony is in decline economically and politically, even while the products of American culture are ubiquitous" (1–2). Detached from political power, the products of US culture can be recontextualized by their consumers around the world. Linking Ekwensu's death with the Wicked Witch suggests that, perhaps, all that's left of the United States is a toxic legacy from which other countries and cultures should detach themselves.

This climactic fight between two ancient spirits at a petrol station funded by Western oil companies offers the flip side of cosmopolitanism: the devouring onslaught of global capitalism. Oil companies have become Ekwensu's tools through the evil of extractive technologies that destroy communities and are toxic to the planet itself. In *Akata Warrior*, this destruction comes to the fore even more. On the TV news one night, Sunny sees an interview with an old man who says that when he moved to the Niger Delta, "there was no crude, no spillage, everything was so fine. People were enjoying back then ... are these oil companies stupid ... don't they know what true wealth is? ... These people aren't from here" (*Warrior* 211). The journalist covering the story talks to a local activist who sets a puddle on fire: "This place is already mutilated by oil pipelines; now the forest and waters are poisoned ... give it a few days and the very *air* will be flammable. We have more than one oil spill every day here ... [and] these oil companies don't care. It's not *their* home" (211–212). Sunny realizes that the "world was literally dying" and then, during another interview in which someone refers to seeing "one big thing wey [sic] be like animal ... like some masquerade tin' ..." (213), Sunny thinks that Ekwensu could easily "tear open a tanker" and bathe in the "freshly spilled crude oil, a substance toxic to the flesh of the earth" (213). These images highlight the connections among racism, capitalism, and environmental disaster.

The contemporary destruction of the environment by the oil companies becomes another of Ekwensu's masquerades, the elaborate masking rituals that are part of Ekpe and West African spiritual practices. What could be more evil and chaotic than making the air itself flammable? To fight Ekwensu, Sunny must develop her own Leopard skills and learn to rely on the skills of her three friends, all Leopards: Chichi and Orlu, who grew up in Nigerian Leopard families, and Sasha, who recently emigrated from the United States to Nigeria with his Leopard family. The four of them become "West Africa's first pre-level *oha* coven," a phrase that Sunny doesn't understand because she didn't grow up in a Leopard community. The coven is a mix of talents and attitudes, Nigerian-born and American-born, male and female. They form a mystical group that "bears the responsibility of the world on its shoulders at a specific point in time" (*Witch* 168). An *oha* coven does not need to be permanent; it forms in response to a particular wickedness and comprises "people of selflessness." A coven must, as Mami says, "serve spirit."

Ekwensu's power is omnidirectional, drawing on whatever it can find to serve its purposes, and the coven must adapt its own powers in order to combat her. When Ekwensu returns, in *Akata Warrior*, the coven must travel to Lagos and win the support of Udide, a giant story-eating spider.[5] In Lagos, the friends spend the night in Victoria Island, a suburb that looks like "the cushiest part of the United States. The houses here were huge and gluttonous . . . the streets were paved and pot-hole free, clean and lined with flowers" (306). Just as Egbunike suggests that we see the Leopards as an indication that Africa can solve its own problems without Anglo-European interference, in the portrayal of Black Hat and the Victoria Island suburb, we see the flip side of that optimism: the local participation in the destruction of the environment and consumption of natural resources. Inside the gated community, Sunny sees a white woman walking a tiny dog and a man in a jogging suit shouting into his phone in Yoruba, the language spoken by the Yoruba tribe. "I'll bet half these people work for the government and oil companies," says Chichi. The devastation caused by the oil companies has been abetted by Nigerians themselves, who reap a profit and then wall themselves away from "Nigeria's many worlds of poverty" (305). Again we see that local allegiances are not always ideal. The inhabitants of Victoria Island seem to have allied themselves with profit rather than with a nurturing sense of place or spirit.

The Leopards are not immune from this self-serving attitude, although Sunny's friends want to believe otherwise. Sasha claims that Leopards are less insular than Lambs because "Leopard People read books by everybody and everything. We look outside *and* inside" (313).

Sasha's point echoes a comment that Orlu has made earlier: "Lambs think money and material things are the most important thing in the world ... Leopard People are different. The only way you can earn *chittim* [magical money] is by *learning*. The more you learn, the more *chittim* you earn" (*Witch* 82). Becoming a good reader—reading books "by everybody"—is crucial to the project of redefining the local. What both Sasha and Orlu overlook is that even the supposedly ideal Leopards can produce people like Black Hat. There is also bias in *Fast Facts for Free Agents*, the book that Sunny relies on to teach her about the Leopard world. Anatov, the coven's teacher, tells her that the author of *Fast Facts* thought that the "truly civilized ideas" came from "Europe and America ... Be aware of her biases toward those not from her homeland" (113). Both Orlu and Sasha are misguided in their attempts to prove that Leopards are somehow more perfect than Lambs: Leopards may be more cosmopolitan than Lambs, but a true Leopard adept will also admit fallibility and weakness.

It is fallibilism that ultimately enables Sunny to win the support of Udide, the spider who lives under the open-air market in Lagos and who challenges Sunny to find a story that she has never heard. It is a daunting task, given that Udide listens to the "millions of stories" in Lagos and many other cities, from New York to Dubai to Rio. All Sunny can do in response is "tell [Udide] my own particular story. It's mine. Only mine. There is only one me ... so maybe yes, this is the only story of its kind" (*Warrior* 335). In honoring her own story as unique and at the same time connecting it to all the other stories on the planet, Sunny situates herself at the intersection of the local— *her* story—and the global—all the other stories in the world. Sunny's story takes place in New York; it is a story of US racism that pits the older African American girls in Sunny's Catholic school against Sunny. She had classmates of all kinds, she says, from African Americans to Muslims, Jews, and Hindus: "[b]ut even though we were all mixed up there, the other kids didn't really mix [and] the African Americans acted like they were kings. And queens." In third grade, Sunny says, she was trapped in the school bathroom by some sixth-grade girls, African Americans who "truly truly hated me" (337). The girls call her a "filthy diseased Shaka Zulu bitch" and mock her albinism. Sunny tries to fight back, calling one of the girls "akata," and pointing out that the girl's period was bleeding through onto her white trousers.

"Akata," Sunny says, "is a word that some said meant cotton picker, others claimed it meant bush animal . . . but a word like that, you don't really need to know what it means . . . it's like a dagger that is a word" (340). In retaliation, the older girls hang her on a coat hook in the bathroom and leave her there.

It is not the tale of Sunny's victimization that wins Udide's support but rather how Sunny explains her actions: "I knew what I'd said was evil. I was American, too. And their history was connected to mine, even if it was not exactly the same . . . I shouldn't have made fun of that girl's shame" (340). And then Sunny goes a step further, enlarging the story beyond her own experience to consider the structures of shame: "Why did they hate me so much. Why? I know why I confuse people. When people are confused, sometimes they get mean and violent" (340). Violence, by this line of reasoning, occurs when categories of understanding are violated, when someone doesn't "belong" or doesn't fit, when someone has, as Sunny terms it, "a defect." Udide says that Sunny's story is "part of a long story of humanity," and while she does not specifically refer to Sunny's apology, it was when Sunny admitted she had made a mistake that Udide's "many hairs rippled."

Fallibilism is a bedrock component of cosmopolitan practice: Admitting that we're wrong is a key step toward engaging with others. In this instance, Sunny's admission illuminates not only the ways in which fear and shame can result in monsterizing, but also the importance of finding points of connection with those who would attempt to Other us. The fact that she and the girl with her period are both physically vulnerable—both subject to shame for their physical bodies—at first sparks Sunny's desire for vengeance and then becomes cause for kinship. Much to her surprise, Sunny has, in fact, found a new story—a story rooted in fallibilism rather than domination.

In the first battle with Ekwensu, Sunny defeats her with Leopard magic and the power of her spirit self, Anyanwu, but in the climactic battle of the second book, Sunny relies on her physical body, not magic. She and Ekwensu are locked in "hand-to-hand combat," an elemental battle. As an albino girl, Sunny has never liked her physical body, despite her prowess as a soccer player. But as she becomes more comfortable in the Leopard world, so too does she become more comfortable with her physical self. The wider world of the Leopards makes her feel less like an oddity, and she begins to take pleasure in her height (she is almost six feet tall) and her strength. She feels "her muscles flex . . . the lean muscles on her arms bulged" (*Warrior* 432) and she rips the mask off Ekwensu, despite having been warned by her misogynist father about the "abomination" of such an act. Sunny breaks convention and thus prevents Ekwensu from creating the "apocalyptic world" that Sunny knows would be inevitable once Ekwensu "really got started" (432). The fact that Sunny beats Ekwensu because she's strong and tenacious is a victory against both environmental apocalypse and gender stereotypes. Learning to take pleasure in her own achievements gives Sunny the wherewithal to understand that "her father's issues weren't hers" (337); she will no longer be constrained by the family narrative of female subservience. The world of the Leopards has rules and constraints, many of which Sunny learns only after she's broken them, but it is also a world that enables gender freedom; the second book ends with Sunny making a brilliant pass on the soccer pitch—the last word of the book is "gooooaallll!"

Sunny defies local Nigerian patriarchy, and at the same time, she challenges the conventions of Leopard culture. After being caught performing magic in front of Lambs, Sunny and the coven are summoned in front of the Library Council, the governing body of the Leopards (and another illustration of the emphasis on reading and education in these speculative novels). As befits a storyteller who won over Udide, Sunny's story to the Council enchants them, even though it challenges the boundaries of their society. The Council is itself a cosmopolitan group, comprised of human and nonhuman shapeshifters who speak multiple languages and resent that they have to speak solely in English because of Sunny's limited Igbo. At the conclusion of the story, the Council is so dazzled by coven exploits—so full of wonder—that there is no punishment. Sunny's abilities as a storyteller lead the Council to bend their much-vaunted rules and to see that what might look like a violation in the abstract was, in practice, the *oha* coven trying to save the world. The coven's actions and Sunny's story have created a new set of narratives, and in so doing, they've found new ways of engaging with the world, locally and beyond-local, in terms of both Lamb society and the spirit world.

The third book in the series, *Akata Woman*, emphasizes the need to find new vantage points on the local. It also reiterates the necessity of being a good reader, of learning to appreciate new stories or old stories told in new ways. At the heart of this novel is a green-glass Möbius-strip ghazal stolen from Udide, who tells Sunny that if the ghazal isn't returned, she will destroy the world. Layered into this quest is the legacy of the Biafra–Nigeria Civil War, Sunny's increasing skill as a reader of Nsibidi script, and her ongoing struggles with her Lamb family—particularly her patriarchal, sometimes violent, father. Even more so than the earlier books in the series, this book stays almost completely focused on Nigeria and its creative energy comes from non-Western sources: The ghazal, for instance, is a complex poetic form that began in seventh-century Arabia and was popularized in medieval Persia by Rumi and Hafiz. Nsibidi script is an equally ancient Nigerian pictograph system, to which Okorafor adds a dollop of magic: The script shape-shifts, so that the book that Sunny reads to practice her Nsibidi skills sometimes takes the form of Sugar Cream's memoir, sometimes a cookbook, sometimes a political satire, sometimes a history of the African continent. Learning to read Nsibidi script is a version of what happens when we read a ghazal (pronounced "guzzle"). Ghazals are written in couplets, each of which ends with the same word or phrase. Depending on the context of the specific couplet, the repeating phrase shifts in meaning; we hold all those meanings in mind simultaneously as we read.

The one powerful exception to the focus on Nigeria here has to do with the legacy of the slave trade, a cultural wound that extends from the Lamb world into the Leopard. During the coven's quest for the ghazal, Sasha stops to make a ceremonial offering at the spot where his ancestors were captured into slavery, a magical ritual that makes his Nigerian-born friends uncomfortable. Sasha challenges their discomfort: "[Y]ou all don't really acknowledge me. I'm American because I'm a descendant of slaves. And no one here talks about that. No one wants to. No big museums, no dedications, nothing" (*Woman* 91). Sasha is the product of several local allegiances—the United States, Nigeria, Igbo, and Leopard—but the power of history extends across all those contexts. As if to drive home the point about that legacy, Okorafor has the four friends "take a knee" in honor of Sasha's commemoration.

This moment of commemoration and grief resounds through the novel in a different and more specifically Nigerian context: the legacy of the Biafra–Nigeria Civil War, which started in 1967, when Biafra seceded from Nigeria in response to Nigerian violence against the Igbo. As the Republic of Biafra, the country struggled to maintain its independence for almost three years, but it was ultimately forced to surrender because the Nigerian blockade of the country led to millions of people dying of starvation. More than fifty years later, the tensions remain: Early in the novel, a pro-Biafra demonstration ends with Orlu's uncle getting killed. The Biafra question extends into the magical world of Ooni, a contiguous universe that Sunny and her friends fall into, where they meet a man named Zed who crashed into Ooni while flying a fighter jet for Biafra. "We could not have won the war," he tells the coven, "but we needed to." Ooni, he explains, is "like Africa if it were never Africa, you know what I mean? Five thousand years from now!" (279). His point echoes what Sasha has said earlier, that it was white colonizers who named "Africa." In this future world, inhabitants live in harmony with the natural world: Zed lives in a baobab tree that has grown into a house, school children are protected by Nchebe Ants, and village houses are made of "braided plants." Zed crashed into this peaceful space and has refused to return to his own world, in which everyone except his wife and sister were killed by Hausa and Fulani in the massacre that sparked the civil war. Through these iterations of violent legacies, both Nigerian and Anglo-European, the novel reminds us that seeing others as monsters—as "them"—leads to destruction and loss.

By means of a magical bridge made of smoke, the coven moves from "living world to spirit world to new living world [to] another level, deeper" (*Woman* 305). The layering of experiences not only enlarges our sense of the local but also reminds us of how we read a ghazal, holding multiple images and contexts in our minds simultaneously. In each world that the coven experiences, they see objects from the other worlds—the Biafran fighter jet in Ooni, a hair comb like the one Sunny left at home on display in the open-air market of Ginen—and in each world, we are asked to consider the relationships between people and environment. Outside Sunny's world of Lamb and Leopard, there is more environmental harmony, from the dwellers in the tree houses to the *papa* stick bug that fastens itself to Orlu's broken arm like a sort of living splint. In the Leopard world, Anatov tells them to become better students of the planet: "[H]uman beings are *notorious* for ignoring the fact that Earth's other creatures are workers of the finest jujus ... you people don't take animals as seriously as you should" (193). Leopards are not exempt from his scolding. Deep in the magical world, Sunny encounters a terrible spirit known as The Bone Collector, who shows her visions of refugees being swallowed by smoke and burning asphalt. The refugees are Biafrans, fleeing Nigerian bombs— but they could just as easily be Syrians, Afghans, Kurds, Ukrainians, or any of the millions of people who have been forcibly displaced by war or climate disasters. Okorafor's trilogy makes clear that both war and climate crisis stem from the legacy of colonialism and unfettered capitalism, which sees the world solely in terms of resources to be exploited.

The bridges in these novels serve as an enactment of Homi Bhabha's metaphor about the "metaphorical fusion of difference [needed] in order to create hybrid new citizens from Benedict Anderson's 'imagined communities'" (qtd. in McCulloch 146). Sunny, Ti-Jeanne, and their communities see themselves as residents not of a nation but of a planet; they "serve spirit." We might, in fact, see cosmopolitanism as the bridge, as an active practice that links disparate individuals and communities through conversation, interaction, and a willingness to move away from the familiar—physically, emotionally, and intellectually. In order to reach "cosmopolitically outwards," as Fiona McCulloch argues, "writers ... must remap geopolitical borders as malleable and fluid" (8). If we can build bridges that help us transcend the limitations of our frequently constraining local allegiances, we can find ways to challenge the singular drive toward profit that results in planetary destruction.

Notes

1. The concept of narco-saint fits in with the *narcocorridos* that El Patrón has written and sung in praise of his power and fame. The *corrida* is a long narrative song that chronicles important moments in Mexican history, a history into which El Patrón hopes to insert himself.

2. The United States ranks among the lowest in the developed world in terms of what it supplies for childcare, according to numerous studies. A 2021 *New York Times* article notes that the United States spends 0.2% of its GDP on childcare for children aged two and under—roughly $500 per child—compared to Norway, which spends close to $30,000 (Miller np).

3. The three women, Hopkinson has said, are feminized versions of the names of the characters in Derek Walcott's play *Ti-Jean and His Brothers*, which provides an

epigraph to her novel. Walcott and Hopkinson's father were friends and artistic collaborators for a period of time, and then had a falling out. Hopkinson explains that "the name Ti-Jean is the French equivalent of 'Everyman.' Early on in the writing of *Brown Girl in the Ring*, I realized it was a novel about three generations of women battling an evil in their lives, and I thought of the parallels with *Ti-Jean and His Brothers*, an early play of Derek's in which three brothers battle the devil. I wanted to acknowledge that connection to Derek's work, so I named the three women Ti-Jeanne, Mi-Jeanne, and Gros-Jeanne—the feminine equivalents of the brothers Ti-Jean, Mi-Jean, and Gros-Jean. I liked the idea of Ti-Jeanne as every-woman. I had to call Derek to ask his permission to quote from the play, and my heart was in my mouth, because I had childhood memories of him and my father shouting in fury at each other. But he was very gracious" (Rutledge 598).

4. Okorafor does not give specifics in Book One, but a 2019 CNN report found that there have been more than 12,000 oil spills in Nigeria between 1974 and 2014, and that more than 40 million liters of crude oil is spilled annually. One of the worst spills, in 2008, was only recently settled; Shell has yet to start cleaning up, claiming that the spill is the result of sabotage (Adebayo np).

5. In a 2017 TedTalk Tanzania, Okorafor refers to Udide the spider, a wise story-teller and the embodiment of the deep roots and untapped sociopolitical power of African science fiction, which, she says, can provide "a will to power." Udide is also the narrator of Okorafor's 2014 novel *Lagoon*, in which mythical deities (including Udide) fight against the destruction of Lagos.

4

Reading Harry Potter in Abu Dhabi

When I first conceived this project, I decided there would not be a separate chapter about *Harry Potter*. Given the ubiquity of the *Potter* books, I thought that perhaps nothing more need be said, other than a few details about their economic clout and perhaps a brief reference to the controversy over J. K. Rowling's comments about trans people. What I failed to take into account are Rowling's readers—my students among them—and the ways in which books might be said to create a sense of the "local" that exists textually rather than geographically. One of my own students reminded me of this fact after a class in which we talked about *The Order of the Phoenix* (2003) and read some of Rowling's comments about trans people. The student asked, with great anxiety, if I still liked the *Potter* books. The anxiety in the student's question didn't seem like something I could chalk up to just economic power or a marketing juggernaut: It sounded more like the student was worried that I was going to scoff at something dear to his heart. I said that yes, I did still like the books, and that they'd brought a lot of people great joy. The student smiled and seemed reassured, but the anxiety-laden question has remained with me.

Despite Rowling's comments, despite the whiteness of the boy wizard's world, those books have a deep hold on the collective imagination, which seems of a piece with what Philip Davis has written about as the mission for this "Literary Agenda" series: "The 'literary' is not pure or specialized or self-confined . . . it consists in what non-writers actively receive from writings when, for example, they start to see the world more imaginatively as a result of reading novels and begin to think more carefully about human personality." What do readers "actively receive" from the *Potter* books, and do these books help us to see the world "more imaginatively"?

Rowling's books have made a huge impact on the lives of their readers, but they've also, of course, made a meteor-sized impact on the publishing world. The books are responsible for the launch, in 2000, of the "children's bestseller" list at *The New York Times*, which effectively removed the *Potter* books from the adult list, where they were blocking "serious" books from making that all-important list: "Authors who would usually find a newly released title in the top ten instead found themselves at #16 or #17, squeezed out of the weekly printed list by the 'Harry Potter effect'" (Fitzsimmons 78). Some literary agents and publishers were delighted by this shift, while others, predictably, were outraged. Regardless of which bestseller list you use, the sales figures for the "Harry Potter" series are astronomical: More than 500 million copies of the book have been sold worldwide; the movie adaptations have made upwards of seven *billion* dollars.

Literary and cultural historians also point to the *Potter* books as making it easier for adults to read "kids' books" in public without apology, thus creating a significant shift in the audience for YA fiction. The shift in the series from "child" to "young adult" happens in sync with Harry's own age: The series takes a more serious turn in *Prisoner of Azkaban*, in which Harry turns thirteen; as a reviewer in *The Guardian* noted, that book is "the last book . . . that feels good to read to most younger children" (Flood np). After the moment in *The Goblet of Fire* when Cedric Diggory—an innocent teenager—is murdered by Voldemort, the books get darker and darker (and longer and longer, another reason they are difficult for younger readers). And yet despite their length and their darkness, and even despite the recent anger over Rowling's comments about trans people, the books continue to sell: They have been translated into more than eighty languages (most recently Scots and Greenlandic), and publishers continue to hope that they will find "the next *Harry*."

It would be difficult, I think, to find anyone over the age of ten who is not familiar with at least the *name* Harry Potter, and there is enough passing familiarity with the arc of the stories that "Potter" functions almost as a kind of lingua franca. Having this touchstone in the classes I've taught at NYU Abu Dhabi (NYUAD) becomes particularly important in the context of NYUAD's deeply international student body. The students at NYUAD come from more than ninety-five countries and speak more than seventy home languages. The language of instruction is English, but because there is no national majority in the classroom, we are all working together toward shared understanding: Every discussion becomes a cosmopolitan exercise, with all its attendant rewards and difficulties. In this context, *Potter* becomes a global text: The students share "the boy who lived," the phrase by which Harry is often characterized, no matter if they've encountered Harry only in the movies, used the books to practice their fluency in another language, read an official translation or a pirated illegal version, or just heard their friends talking about wands and Quidditch.

Our discussions in class are about the content of the books, but they are also about translation and what it means that *Potter* has come to their countries while books in their home languages have not circulated into Harry's world of the United Kingdom or the United States.[1] The *Potter* books offer a way to talk about conceptions of world literature and students' own educational experiences, including their experiences of reading, which includes—almost always—issues of censorship. The near-complete universality of the books also enables us to talk about what it means to have this cosmopolitan reading experience, which is simultaneously local and global: What does it mean to have read the unofficial Arabic translation at night by iPhone flashlight, and how might that resonate with someone who read the same book in a Slovenian translation as part of a mother–daughter book group? These specific local differences enable students to think in very concrete ways about how context contributes to understanding and perception. The *Potter* series offers us the opportunity to think about the cosmopolitanism *in* the books, but also allows us to talk about the cosmopolitanism of readership and circulation.

Over and over again, regardless of where the students grew up or their home language, they refer to the *Potter* books as giving them a haven, offering them an imaginative space to call their own. A student once went so far as to say that the books had shaped his entire personality, and another said that it's possibly more common to know about Harry than it is to have access to clean water. The haven that these books provide to their readers is interestingly self-referential because the series is, in many ways, precisely *about* reading. From the inexorable deluge of Hogwarts admissions letters in the first book to the fairy tales, fake news, and history books of the final novel, *Potter* wants us to read, and read well. Books in the series possess their readers, attack their readers, trick their readers; books are soul-stealers and soul-keepers, and reading well, as Hermione does, time and again, becomes one of the key weapons against the tyranny of Voldemort.

And yet at the same time, the series also illustrates something that perhaps we know instinctively when we are young and then lose sight of: Reading can be dangerous. It takes us out of own lives, which may speak to why children's books so often turn up on lists of banned books and why grown-ups (parents, teachers, librarians) try to put guidelines and boundaries around what is or is not appropriate for young readers. Harry's efforts to make meaning from the texts that surround him—aided always by the indefatigable and brilliant Hermione—embody one of the ideas central to Appiah's conception of cosmopolitanism: "[E]valuating stories together is one of the central human ways of learning to align our responses to the world. And that alignment of responses is, in turn, one of the ways we maintain the social fabric, the texture of our relationships" (*Cosmopolitanism* 29). The *Potter* series, like so much YA fiction, enables its audience to consider itself as readers and to find power in that position; the books are almost a meta-commentary on readership, textual autonomy, and critical thinking—lessons that Rowling herself, in her public statements, seems to have forgotten.

Jack Zipes, the eminent scholar of children's literature and fairy tales, sees Rowling's books as rehashings of old stories that don't warrant the accolades they've received. He says that "what distinguishes the plots of Rowling's novels, however, are their conventionality, predictability, and happy ends despite the clever turns of phrases and surprising twists in the intricate plots. They are easy and delightful to read, carefully manicured and packaged, and they sell extraordinarily well precisely because they are so cute and ordinary" (Woodward np). The boy wizard is a focus of Zipes's 2001 book, *Sticks and Stones: The Troublesome Success of Children's Literature from Slovenly Peter to Harry Potter*, in which Zipes says that it is precisely the wild success of the *Potter* books that makes it difficult for anyone to take the books seriously (171–172). This attitude seems like a throwback to a view of "serious literature" that regards with suspicion any writer who actually sells books: The more books you sell, the worse the books must be.

What Zipes and others seem to overlook are the ways that the *Potter* books dramatize the power of reading—including, as Elizabeth Teare notes in a 2002 essay, an ongoing reckoning with the commodification of reading and literary celebrity.[2] In *The Chamber of Secrets*, after all, one of the villains is Gilderoy Lockhart, a heartthrob celebrity author whose books are all fakes and whose cowardice almost gets Harry, Ginny, and Ron killed. Other examples of dangerous texts abound: the monster book in *The Prisoner of Azkaban* that will bite its readers unless it is approached correctly; the Marauder's Map that can only be read if the appropriate incantation is murmured; the diary of Tom Riddle that possesses Ginny Weasley in a dark manifestation of being "lost in a book"; the annotations in the book of potions that put Harry in danger in *The Half-Blood Prince*. Rowling's series repeatedly warns us about the danger of celebrity authorship, the risk of bad reading, and the ease with which media can become a tool of tyrants. Zipes is right that the books are commodities; we cannot ignore that fact. At the same time, we can think about all the ways that people circumvent the power of the marketplace: writing and sharing fan fiction, handmade PDF copies, chapbooks, and so forth. We can also recognize that there is a distinction to be made between the experience of buying and reading a book and that of buying a length of garden hose at the local hardware store.

Books are commodities, that's true, but it is also true that when we choose to read outside the texts that have been made available to us, books can become a way to resist authority. Some of my students talk about sharing *Potter* books *samizdat*-style, passing around illicit translations or forbidden copies of dog-eared editions. The series highlights the risks of illicit reading, most particularly in *Order of the Phoenix*, where to be caught reading the wrong sort of book by Dolores Umbridge or her minions is to risk extreme physical punishment. "Umbridge reminds me of my school," said a student who grew up in Taiwan. "Like, there were things we weren't supposed to read, and we would get in trouble if we got caught." Another student nodded in agreement and told us about the librarian at her school in Qatar who loaned students her copy of *The Diary of Anne Frank*, which she kept wrapped in brown paper behind her desk. And yet another student talked about seeing posters for "Harry Potter" movies where she grew up in a suburb of Colorado Springs, but that she wasn't able to read the books or see the movies until she got to college because she was home-schooled and Rowling was not on her parents' curriculum. "The thing is," said the Taiwanese student, "reading can be dangerous. It can be really risky, and depending on the government . . ." She didn't finish the sentence, but the rest of the class understood what she was talking about. The class had arrived together at an awareness articulated by the editors of *ELH*: "If a book is not an innocuous object, neither is reading (it) an innocent practice. Reading cannot be taken for granted, either in the material sense of who can do it under what conditions or in the technical sense of what constitutes and counts as reading" (Slaughter 318). My students are aware that who gets to read what is something to be noticed and valued. They see this same awareness in the *Potter* books, which is one reason so many of them found room for their experiences in Harry's world, despite the material differences in their circumstances.

What strikes me, as I consider the conversations I've had about *Harry Potter* over the past decade with my NYUAD students, is how often students connect across their different local experiences of the books by finding commonalities in their experiences of censorship. In these conversations about textual policing, there is never a suggestion that *this* kind of policing was better than *that* kind, or that this country's policies were better than that country's policies. Instead, what emerged was a discussion about how the rhetoric of "safety" took on different shapes and valences in different contexts, and the ease with which such rhetoric takes root. The *Potter* books give them ways to think about what they've seen happening in their communities because the series enacts the gradual suppression of a free press. The process is played for laughs in *The Goblet of Fire*, when Rita Skeeter tries to create a scandal about Harry and his "love interests." But in *The Order of the Phoenix*, the destructive power of fake news is no longer a joke and the ways in which the press manipulates—and is manipulated— becomes a bleak symbol of authoritarian power. In *Deathly Hallows*, the only real source of information is the underground radio show "Potterwatch," which broadcasts in defiance of Voldemort and the Ministry of Magic.[3] All of these iterations of a corrupt press and the risk of flouting an authoritarian government seem very real to my students, many of whom come from countries in which all media is controlled by the State. When I first started teaching the *Potter* books, my US students extolled the freedom of the press enjoyed by the US media, but in 2022, almost no US student feels confident about such a claim.

Potter, as many scholars have noted, has a great deal to say about nationalism and ethnicity: The series as a whole is very much against the idea that "purity" is a key to the well-being of the State. Harry's mother is "Muggle-born," as is Voldemort's father, which is why Voldemort (still Tom Riddle at that point) kills him and the rest of his family. Hermione's parents are Muggles as well, and in order to protect them from Voldemort's wrath, Hermione orphans herself, sending her parents away and erasing their memories of her. It seems a high price to pay, and we never learn if she reconnects with them after Voldemort is defeated and order restored. All the books illustrate, with increasing degrees of intensity, the seductive promise of cultural purity, which seems to offer certainty and clearly drawn boundaries. But it also becomes clear that these boundaries lock us in; the barriers are only necessary if you're afraid of what's on the other side, if you're afraid of affiliating beyond what you know about yourself. Fear leads to a desire for control, as we see in the annotated potions in the book that Harry finds in *The Half-Blood Prince*. It is Hermione, always a good reader, who does not trust the spells. She recognizes that the potions have the same consequences as spells used by Death Eaters: "dangling people in the air. Making them float along, asleep, helpless" (*Half-Blood Prince* 241). Later, in the sessions that Harry has with Dumbledore over the Pensieve, Dumbledore points out that Riddle's tendency was to use magic "against other people, to frighten, to punish, to control" (276). Dumbledore tells Harry that the Horcrux that Voldemort had embedded in the diary that possessed Ginny in *The Chamber of Secrets* was there because Voldemort wanted to be "read, wanted the piece of his soul to inhabit or possess somebody else" (*Half-Blood Prince* 501). Voldemort is a writer who won't allow his readers the luxury of interpretation; he wants to impose certainty and always be at the epistemological center.

The cosmopolitanism in Rowling's books (as opposed to their function as global texts) rests in the willingness of the "good guys" to create community across species—a giant, a werewolf, a centaur, even the giant spider Aragog is tolerated (Harry goes with Hagrid to help bury the spider and says a few words at the spider's death in *The Half-Blood Prince*). At the center of these novels are mixed-blood

Harry and Muggle-born Hermione, whose actions rely on collaboration, a willingness to accept diversity, and what Appiah would call "contamination." Appiah reminds us that our connections to local communities are as much a product of our imaginations as are our connections to larger abstractions, like nation or State: "[T]he connection through local identity is as imaginary as the connection through humanity ... but this isn't to pronounce either of them unreal. They are among the realest connections we have" (*Cosmopolitanism* 135). It is the power of imagination to establish connections that Voldemort lacks. Dumbledore tells Harry that the greatest power of all is love, but the series makes a strong case that the second greatest is imagination. In the "King's Cross" chapter of *Deathly Hallows*, as Harry prepares to go back to the land of the living after letting himself be killed by Voldemort, he asks Dumbledore, "Is this real? Or has this been happening inside my head?" Dumbledore replies, "Of course it is happening inside your head, Harry, but why on earth should that mean that it is not real?" (*Deathly Hallows* 723). Dumbledore easily sees that the imaginary can be real, but Voldemort cannot imagine anything outside himself. He cannot imagine the love of a parent for a child, for example, which is why he is defeated by Lily Potter and betrayed by Narcissa Malfoy; he cannot imagine someone like Neville Longbottom—a pure-blood—choosing to side with the impure. Like tyrants of all sorts, mortal and magical, Voldemort knows only one story, and within that story, he's always the central character, always the center of certainty.

The ability to imagine beyond the self and to acknowledge the connections between self and other are so much at the heart of the *Harry Potter* novels that it may explain the global outrage that greeted Rowling's comments about trans women, which seemed very much at odds with the principles of the Potterverse.[4] In her comments about trans people, Rowling insists on an essentialist definition of "woman," writing on her personal website:

> I want trans women to be safe. At the same time, I do not want to make natal girls and women less safe. When you throw open the doors of bathrooms and changing rooms to any man who believes or feels he's a woman—and, as I've said, gender confirmation certificates may now be granted without any need

for surgery or hormones — then you open the door to any and
all men who wish to come inside. That is the simple truth.

(10 June 2020)

In this same piece, Rowling referenced her experiences as a sexual
assault survivor "not to garner sympathy," but to explain why she
feels so strongly that "natal women" need a place where they can feel
safe from aggressive men. In an essay from later that same summer
(August 2020), Rowling explained that she was returning the "Ripple
of Hope" award given to her by the Robert F. Kennedy Foundation in
2019 because Kerry Kennedy, president of the Foundation, had made
a statement condemning Rowling's views on trans people and calling
her transphobic. Rowling writes, "As a longstanding donor to LGBT
charities and a supporter of trans people's right to live free of perse-
cution, I absolutely refute the accusation that I hate trans people or
wish them ill, or that standing up for the rights of women is wrong,
discriminatory, or incites harm or violence to the trans community"
(Rowling 2020). She goes on to say that given the "very serious conflict
of views" between herself and the Foundation, she has no choice but
to return the award.

Rowling's comments about trans people seemed to many readers to
contradict the messages of her novels, and they also demonstrate the
difficulty of maintaining a cosmopolitan practice. These statements
testify to *Rowling's* belief that she is a progressive-minded liberal cosmopolitan, but her actions suggest otherwise. There appears to be
some innate set of beliefs at work that preclude conversation or exchange: She gives the award back; sends the mocking tweet; writes
the vaguely self-serving essay. And so as readers, we are presented
with a dilemma that in turn tests our *own* cosmopolitan practices: Do
we dismiss Rowling and her work entirely? Can we find ways to bal-
ance our responses in order to ask questions that might allow us to find
a way to establish connections and understanding, while also pushing
at the boundaries of interpretation in order to expand our structures
of feeling?

When we read *Jane Eyre*, for example, we realize that on the one
hand, Charlotte Brontë was wildly progressive in creating the figure of
Jane, a woman who insisted on her own agency and subjectivity. And,
on the other hand, we note that Brontë could not imagine the figure of

Rochester's first wife, a woman from the Caribbean, as being anything other than a beast. Antoinette Cosway as written in *Jane Eyre* has no humanity, and it took Jean Rhys, herself from Dominica, to "give the poor lunatic a voice" and write back against Brontë's Anglocentricism, in *Wide Sargasso Sea* (1966). We don't toss *Jane Eyre* into the garbage (I hope not, anyway), but we don't accept Brontë's description of the "mad woman" either.

A student offered this insightful comment about how Rowling's comments would impact their reading in the future: "[T]he dilemma of the author and her text ... can only be answered through an attempt, a promise that we as readers will celebrate the preserved literary art of a fallen author while discerning the bias planted in her tracks." Another student ruefully noted that Rowling's statements put him in the position of being "too young to fully grapple with the death of the author but too old to believe in magic." As readers, they are learning how to navigate between author and text—and ironically, they may have, at least in part, gained a sense of their authority as readers from reading *Harry Potter*. In much of the commentary about Rowling's statements about trans people, the dismay is expressed in almost familial terms, which makes sense when we consider how many people say they "grew up" with *Harry Potter*. "Rowling is like my super-religious aunt," a student said. "I love my aunt, but her views about gay people are terrible, and if she knew I was gay, it would be really bad. But she's old and I love my family so ..." He shrugged. Another student chimed in about Rowling: "Exactly. I am who I am because of her, but now I have to stop listening to her, and just listen to the books." Crazy Aunt Jo could have her tirades, it seemed; they just weren't going to listen to her anymore.

These students, across their diverse upbringings and insights, were not ready to jettison the haven that *Potter* had provided for them. They could, in one way or another, see themselves as Harry or Hermione (and even a few as Ron): not as wizards, but as, perhaps, queer kids in religiously conservative families or societies; kids who wanted to write or paint rather than study engineering or physics; kids whose siblings were "successful" while they were not; girls who wanted to be Hermiones instead of wives. The ways they discussed *Potter* illustrate what I mean by cosmopolitanism as a practice: Despite the material differences in how they encountered the *Potter* books, they found ways to talk to each other about their experience. They were curious, engaged, respectful. As the students negotiate the layers of diversity that exist in the classrooms of NYUAD—diversity of language, ethnicity, religion, class, race—they find ways to engage: There are convergences from which we can begin to build layers of connection that bridge our differences.

Even before the controversy about trans people erupted, students found that the *Potter* novels gave them the opportunity to grapple with social and cultural issues. Citing Christine Schoefer's 2000 essay, "Harry Potter's Girl Trouble," I point out that girls "have an uncanny ability to imagine themselves in male roles" a skill that has been honed on "virtually all children's literature as well as Hollywood's younger audience films" (np). Boys, on the other hand, are rarely asked to make this crossing; they have the freedom to "dissociate from the limitations of female characters" (np). As you might imagine, the boys protest the validity of this generalization—but few of them could cite more than *The Hunger Games* as an example of something they've read with a female protagonist. Girls, on the other hand, regardless of where they grew up, nod in recognition at the idea of reading with this dual consciousness. And yet none of the students wanted to admit that the gender politics of Harry's world were retrograde: "Girls, when they are not downright silly or unlikable, are helpers, enablers and instruments. No girl is brilliantly heroic the way Harry is, no woman is experienced and wise like Professor Dumbledore" (Schoefer, "Girl Trouble" np). Saying such a thing seemed to the students somehow disloyal, an admission that the wizarding world was more like ours than they wanted it to be. Schoefer's essay was published before the series concluded and, as students always hasten to point out, Hermione becomes increasingly central—"She's like the fixer," a student once said, "the savior of the savior." The students don't want the gender politics of the novel to be a reflection of the world in which they live—it's as if they can separate Rowling from her books, but they do not want to be critical of the texts themselves.

Until, that is, we arrive at the epilogue of *Deathly Hallows*, which sits at the end of the series like an uneasily perched lid trying to tamp down something that does not want to be contained. The epilogue attempts to corral a sprawling saga into a tidy "happily ever after," a goal at odds with the inventiveness of the series itself. In fairy tales—which is what *Potter* is, at its base—the happily ever after arrives as a heteronormative coupling after some rather dramatic bloodshed: The wicked queen in Grimm's "Snow White," for instance, is made to dance at Snow White's wedding in red-hot iron shoes until she falls down dead. Rowling contains the death and bloodshed to the narrative itself—the death of Fred Weasley and the battle between Mrs. Weasley and Bellatrix Lestrange—while the epilogue is all gentleness and suburban normalcy: Harry finally achieves his heart's desire which, let's face it, is not that exciting. All he's ever wanted is a family, stability, security, love—desires so ordinary that Voldemort finds them unfathomable. Harry doesn't have his parents, but he *is* a parent, intent on giving his children what he didn't have. The wit of the earlier books is absent from the epilogue, as is any reference to texts or reading, as if in this staid post-Voldemort world, we have no use for complex texts or astute readers. All the characters are married off, with the exception of Neville, now a professor of Herbology and the only character who could almost have been Harry, had Voldemort chosen to attack Neville's parents instead of Harry's. Neville is the hero of the Battle of Hogwarts, inheritor of Godric Gryffindor's sword, slayer of Nagini, and pure-blood resistor of Voldemort's blandishments—he is, in some ways, much more interesting than Harry. Neville works with plants, and I imagine that he might be the only person at Hogwarts to think about climate crisis; I could imagine him hanging out with the Mushroom Master or planting crops with the community at Acorn.

After this overly tidy conclusion, Rowling blew it all up several months later by saying at a public lecture that of course she'd always imagined Dumbledore as gay. The relationship between Dumbledore and Gellert Grindelwald is ostensibly at the heart of the "Fantastic Beasts and Where to Find Them" film franchise (for which Rowling gets co-writing credit), and yet, as fans are pointing out with increasing irritation, there is no actual *relationship*, other than vague implications, "exemplified by such unsatisfactory touches as a single, longing glance in a mirror in 'The Crimes of Grindelwald'" (Bundel np). It seems almost as if Rowling wants to make the wizarding world more diverse than it actually is, but she can't quite get there. Like Brontë and her madwoman, Rowling can stretch her cosmopolitan vision only so far; she can't quite relinquish her entrenched views.

It is an interesting irony: Rowling perhaps cannot imagine trans women as women; she cannot write scenes in which Dumbledore passionately embraces another man; she imagines only the most conventional of endings for her wildly inventive series. And yet in creating the series, she has enabled her readers to imagine all those things, to change their own structures of feeling so that they can find a safe haven in her books and find connections with those whose differences seem insurmountable. When I think about the fact that so many of my students—so many people in the world—have encountered *Potter* in translation, we see that the books offer space for transformation. Susan Friedman's comment about what she calls "translational migrations" is useful in this regard:

> The very gap between languages ... is a space for intercultural encounter, for the crossing over, even for the productive transgression of purity. In short, translation from one language to another invites the fraught, difficult, but potentially enriching process of cultural translation. Translation is more than the "crossing over" from one language to another; it is also the crisscrossing, the intersections, the intermingling of different cultural values, belief and affect systems, and modes of understanding and communication.
>
> (23)

The *Potter* books thus seem to offer a "local" to their readers, particularly, perhaps, those readers who grew up with family histories of displacement, migration, and diaspora, as well as readers who consider themselves the product of multiple identities. In this crisscrossing, *Potter* readers (young and old) may find a rooted space from which they can imagine outward, seeing alternative possibilities to their own lives and social structures.

The series provides models of coalition-building in the face of an existential threat to the world, and while the threat here is Voldemort rather than climate change, the impact is similar. The affiliative communities that spring up through and across the novels belie the heteronormative epilogue, but they are essential to the "Fantastic Beasts" series. When we look past the drama about the nature of Dumbledore's desire, we see how Rowling's magical world may be reckoning with environmental crisis: Newt Scamander is a "magizoologist" who wants to save various magical creatures from extinction. In another of the series' many meta-commentaries about books and reading, *Fantastic Beasts and Where to Find Them* was published as a stand-alone book that purported to be written by Newt Scamander and was made to look like the textbook used by Harry in *Harry Potter and the Philosopher's Stone* (the title appears on Harry's first-ever list of textbooks needed for Hogwarts). Newt's love of creatures echoes Anatov's admonition to Sunny and the coven about learning from the animals of the world in *Akata Witch*; it may be that the final lesson of the Potterverse will be about establishing new ways to engage with the planet.

The success of the *Potter* books has given rise to an extraordinary amount of scholarly work—an entire field now exists called "Potter Studies," for example—and yet this abundance does not give the full picture. Most of the scholarly work exists within the realm of children's literature and/or pedagogy studies, as a quick search of academic journals over the past twenty years illustrates: A keyword search of "Harry Potter" turns up about four thousand articles, almost all of which are tagged with words like education, children's literature, pedagogy, language arts. That is to say, Rowling's work still gets short shrift in more mainstream publications and in scholarly work about "grown-up" books. For example, A. S. Byatt wrote in *The New York Times* in 2003 that

> Ms. Rowling's world has no place for the numinous. It is written for people whose imaginative lives are confined to TV cartoons and the exaggerated (more exciting, not threatening) mirror-worlds of soaps, reality TV and celebrity gossip. ... Nobody is trying to save or destroy anything beyond Harry Potter and his friends and family.
>
> (np)

Byatt was writing before the series had concluded, and her accusations of smallness are reframed by Michiko Kakutani, who, in her review of *Deathly Hallows*, observes that Harry's world is "perfectly recognizable to readers, a place where death and the catastrophes of daily life are inevitable, and people's lives are defined by love and loss and hope—the same way they are in our own mortal world" (np). Kakutani, like Byatt, sees the mundane in Harry's world, but unlike Byatt, she sees that mimetic quality as something to praise rather than condemn. Given the commercial power of *Deathly Hallows*, which broke sales records for the most books sold in a twenty-four-hour period, it seems inevitable that Kakutani—then the most important reviewer in the United States—would review the book, but it is attitudes like Byatt's that seem to have prevailed.

In John Sutherland's *Little History of Literature* (2013), published by Yale University Press, Rowling is invoked as a writer who "made it," in tones that can best be described as snarky:

> When writers are lucky enough to go global, they can earn amounts that rival the revenues of a multinational company. J.K. Rowling, for example, was listed in 2013 as the thirtieth richest person in the UK (and unique, among this select group, in that every penny of her wealth was earned, not inherited). She's not as rich as Coca-Cola, but *Harry Potter* is read in as many places as that fine drink is drunk.
>
> (244)

In this comparison, *Potter* becomes the textual equivalent of a fizzy, sugary drink that's been proven to be bad for your health.

Less snarky but equally dismissive is Rebecca Walkowitz's reference to Rowling in a 2007 essay, "Unimaginable Largeness: Kazuo Ishiguro, Translation, and the New World Literature." Walkowitz observes that

> because a text's network will continue to grow and multiply, as that text is circulated and read in numerous regions and languages, its geography and culture will be dynamic and unpredictable. It is no longer simply a matter of determining, once and for all, the literary culture to which a work belongs ... In other words, because works can continue to become part of different national traditions, there will always be more comparing to do.
>
> (217)

Given what we've seen about how Rowling's books circulate in the world, it seems unsurprising that Walkowitz makes reference to her work: "Let us for a moment think of Ishiguro alongside J. M. Coetzee, and even J. K. Rowling: all three writers know that the books they are producing will circulate beyond a single nation and in near-immediate translation into many languages" (220). Coetzee and Ishiguro become key discussions in the rest of Walkowitz's essay; Rowling is relegated to a footnote. Walkowitz concedes that Rowling's novels "contribute to linguistic diversity, even if this was not their author's chief intention. Of course, the value and consequence of linguistic diversity should not be taken for granted. Variation is not in itself democratic or liberal if the demand for authenticity and distinctiveness restricts freedom rather than facilitates it" (Walkowitz 100). As so often happens in discussions of "kids' books," the question of audience gets elided, as does the power of their reading experience. In her glancing reference to "even" Rowling, Walkowitz dismisses the idea that these books, in whatever language, seem to offer their readers precisely a space of freedom, where they can explore and examine their own worlds and the world around them.

A recent study of reading patterns in Israel offers an example of how reading Rowling in translation creates a kind of freedom, a loosening of the ties of national identity. The researchers looked at three different communities, which they characterized as "veteran secular Jews, Russian immigrant Jews, and Arabs." The study found that

> in all three ethno-cultural communities, reading publics read translations of classic world literature and modern bestsellers, and intellectual elites also read books in English ... a body of some shared knowledge did emerge, though limited. These shared contents seemed to neglect ethnic and national issues, instead focusing on individuals' needs and fulfillment, environmental issues, and universal human problems. Books by José Saramago, Haruki Murakami, and J.K. Rowling, [were] mentioned by well-read people from the three communities.
>
> (Adoni and Nossek 71)

Rowling keeps good company here, but it seems important to note that, in distinction to Walkowitz's claim, reading in translation moved readers away from the claims of nation and ethnicity, with all the conflict and animosity those claims might connote in the context of Israel, and instead brought their attention to the environment and the larger human community.

Walkowitz claims that Rowling's books do not do what Ishiguro's work does, which is to "present global comparison as *story* and *discourse*, as something that characters do to assess the value and consequence of their actions, and as something that readers do—or need to do— to reflect on those assessments and to consider the various ways that value and consequence can be determined" (223, italics in original). I do not want to suggest that Rowling's writing works at the same level as Ishiguro's, but I do think that this description represents a misreading of Rowling's books, which, as I have argued, are quite self-consciously aware of the circulation of stories and the way those stories shape not only our actions, but also how we reflect, value, and assess those actions. The fact that global audiences can access these ideas in their own languages seems significant, particularly because the novels dramatize the importance of becoming a good reader, which in another self-referential spin, suggests that people reading *Potter* in translation need to think about why it is that texts come out of English into other languages but not as readily in the other direction. Friedman points out that "the space of translation brings differences into some kind of relation or conversation, out of which the potential exists (not always fulfilled) for the pursuit of greater understanding and coexistence. In this sense, the translational is a site of dynamic, situated cosmopolitanisms" (23). As a global text, then, *Potter* demands that we think about the very structure of "global" and about what it is we mean when we talk about "world literature." Rowling's novels give more power to her readers than perhaps she knew—a manifestation of precisely what happens *in* the novels, as text after text eludes its author and becomes something else in the hands and minds of good readers.

Notes

1. Gillian Lathey notes that "research into global translation traffic indicates that there is a significant imbalance between translations into and from the English language. Recent sociological interpretations of international exchange include those of Johan Heilbron (2010) who posits a hierarchical system that governs world translation flows, with English currently in a central position as the source language for the world's published translations; or Pascale Casanova's (2007) political view of inequality and power struggle that identifies dominating and dominated languages, with English in the dominating category" (42). Citing Laurence Venuti's comment that the inequity of translations is "embarrassing" because of what it indicates about a kind of cultural hegemony, Lathey cites a 2012 study that bears out her claims:

"a statistical report on all translated literature in the UK and Ireland compiled by Jasmine Donahaye of Swansea University in 2012 suggests that just 3 percent of all publications is the likely figure for the proportion of translated books in the sample years of 2000, 2005 and 2008" (Donahaye qtd. in Lathey 43).

2. Teare's essay is included in *Ivory Tower and Harry Potter: Perspectives on a Literary Phenomenon* (2002).

3. While Rowling could never have planned such a thing, it seems worthy of note that "critics of the [Thai] monarchy . . . voice[d] their concerns publicly in a protest event where they donned outfits to resemble characters from Harry Potter" (np). The commodity becomes transformed by its users into something unexpected and yet, at the same time, something that very much fits the spirit of the final books in the series, as Harry and his compatriots fight against an imperial enemy (Sombatpoonsiri 5).

4. For a representative view, see Aja Romano's piece in *Vox* (2020) or Dawn Ennis in *Forbes* (2019).

Conclusion

As I was finishing this book, *The New York Times* ran a series of articles about the frustrations experienced by climate scientists who are sure that the world is not running out of time to do something about climate crisis but is in fact *out* of time. If we don't relearn our habits, reorganize our ways of thinking about the world and our relationship to that world, if we don't imagine new structures of feeling that enable us to see human and nonhuman in connection instead of seeing that-which-is-not-us as competition or commodity, we are, effectively, doomed. We will become the first species to self-extinguish—and there will be very few of us left to appreciate the irony. In his weekly newsletter, American environmentalist Alex Steffen writes that "we have never needed new thinking more . . . . We need thousands upon thousands of committed people learning how to lead in the real world of un-precedented and uncontrolled change, and finding ways to leverage opportunity and impact together" ("We're Not yet Ready" np). Steffen may be thinking in terms of public policy and advocacy, but creative work is also essential, particularly for those who think about their work the way Hopkinson does: "[H]ow can I cause myself, and the reader, to see things differently? What can I do to challenge, delight, surprise, unsettle?" (Johnston 206).

Hopkinson's question anticipates what Ebony Thomas calls for in *The Dark Fantastic* about the need for new stories that will destabilize silencing and totalizing hierarchies. Sometimes, as in the case of the "Nsibidi Scripts" series, these new stories are old stories being told to a new audience. Thomas notes that: "[D]ecolonizing our fantasies and our dreams . . . means liberating magic itself. For resolving the crisis of race in our storied imagination has the potential to make our world anew" (169). Although Thomas doesn't say so explicitly, embedded in this remaking of the world is the need to address climate crisis and find alternative ways of engaging with the world. We might think about the reminder that Anatov gives the *oha* coven in *Akata Woman* about taking animals "seriously," a reminder that culminates in the coven learning about magical movement from a gecko. Magical movement may be outside our own lived experience, but we can still take from Anatov's comment the importance of seeing animals (and the nonhuman world) not as commodities but as teachers—as equal inhabitants on the planet.

Can YA fiction help to unsettle—and delight—the young adults who are coming of age now, in the third year of a pandemic and as Russian invades Ukraine in a terrible illustration of the destructive power of nationalism coupled with capitalism? Steffen holds out a small gesture of hope that dovetails with the project of speculative YA fiction, when he calls for "an intellectual and creative leap into engagement with the realities of our transapocalyptic present. If we are not foolish, we will be learning more, listening more, helping more, sharing more, engaging more . . . Because on a small planet, no one else's crisis is theirs alone. Denial is a flimsy wall, and border walls and sea walls will not prove much stronger. Connection is the only effective strategy" ("Transapocalyptic Now"). Making those connections, as we have seen, is at the heart of the YA literature that I have discussed in this book. And in turn, the connections forged in these books offer us imaginative possibilities for how to reckon with climate crisis and other existential threats through realignments of our relationships to one another and the planet.

On a structural level, these novels remind us that becoming a good reader, one who is not afraid of ambiguity or complexity, is a necessity for anyone who hopes to navigate a changing world—or who wants to avoid being manipulated into violence, like the followers of Gideon in Roanhorse's *Storm of Locusts* or Andrew Jarret in Butler's *Parable* books. Reading beyond the seductive simplicity of a single story, finding connections to stories that aren't necessarily "ours," becomes the first step toward resisting fundamentalist attitudes toward people and planet. In *Akata Woman*, for example, Sunny tells Orlu that she learned a bit about Biafra from Nigerian Americans but she also "read up on it . . . I got sick of not understanding the context of stuff" (44). Becoming a good reader, in other words, necessitates learning about context, or context*s*, rather than accepting a single story or single history.

This mode of reading, which I characterize as a cosmopolitan reading practice, is one of the cosmopolitanisms at work in these novels. When we learn to hold multiple interpretations in mind, as Alif does, for example, we gain a wider understanding of the world. Connections, rather than divisions, come into focus. That ability, in turn, helps guard against seeing difference or conflict as monstrous. Instead, we see the threat posed by the monsters of commodification, extractive technologies, capitalism. Ekwensu's manipulation of oil companies or The Bone Collector appearing in a miasma of burning asphalt in Okorafor's world; El Patrón's endless consumption of bodies in Farmer's: These are the monsters that we need to fear, even as these monsters attempt to cloak their behaviors through inculcating fear–fear of the mixed-race, the spirits, the nonhuman.

The seeming threat of the monster is the way it destabilizes our categories of knowing and threatens our sense of ourselves; the identities of the monster and the monstrous are fluid, malleable, depending on context. It makes sense, then, that so much of YA fiction occupies itself with monsters, because adolescents are, themselves, fluid; they exist in a liminal state whose boundaries may not be the same from culture to culture, family to family. When we read YA from the vantage point of adulthood, we reinhabit that fluid moment and thus, if we are open to the possibilities, we can see ourselves and our adult lives differently. "Cross-reading," as Rachel Falconer calls it, highlights "how children's literature has never existed in a truly separate sphere … Cross-reading is another of the ways in which we become, in Kristeva's phrase 'strangers to ourselves'" (9). Cross-reading becomes a way of reading across time, putting ourselves in the position of our younger selves, even if those younger selves are in fact inhabiting some future world. Doing this reading not only enables us to re-examine our own histories as readers but also enables us to imagine modes of engaging with the world that are different from our quotidian adult realities.

Stepping outside ourselves also enables us to examine our allegiance to the local, to the systems of belief and behavior that we assume to be "natural" or "universal," or even "just the way things are." We may find, in fact, that these local allegiances have been formed as a reaction against some perceived monster but are in fact serving as constraints that prevent us from making changes to our surroundings. Through the double distancing of "speculative" and "YA," we see ourselves and our relationships to the world differently; we are "unsettled," to use Hopkinson's word. This ironic distance works in several ways: We see the cosmopolitanisms that are at work *in* the texts (the alliances across species, the formation of affiliative communities) and then we also see how cosmopolitanisms can work in terms of audience and reception, as in the case of *Harry Potter* or the "Nsibidi Scripts" series, which to religious conservatives in Nigeria register as "superstition and witchcraft" (Alter np). It is precisely these sorts of local constraints that Okorafor's series—and Rowling's, and the other novels that I have discussed here—are working against.

And yet as we see with *Harry Potter*, these novels can also offer their readers a version of the local—imagined and yet embodied through reading—and from that local, different global connections can be made. Like the old saying goes, think global, act local—an idea that Edmond Totin, a climate scientist has taken to heart: "I make more impact at the local level than the higher level . . . I don't even believe I make any change at the global level" (Zhong np). The example of Farmer's Matt Alacran may be heartening here: The powerful social transformations that occur within the local space of Opium will, ultimately, shape the larger world outside Opium's borders once the local changes take hold. We might also think about the slow progress of Butler's Earthseed, which shifts local attitudes bit by bit and then launches itself into space. The local impacts the global if and when we can make changes in the local that foster connections outside and across seemingly inexorable boundaries.

All of these elements—cosmopolitan reading, affiliating with the monster, remapping the local—help to dismantle the hierarchical structures that have enabled centuries of environmental destruction. YA speculative fiction gives us the tools with which to imagine new possibilities and new ways of thinking, and yet it is work that does not often come into the conversations around climate change and climate crisis—even though the targeted readership for these novels will inherit these seemingly intractable problems. The cultural work being done by YA fiction creates opportunities for us to think about radical restructurings of our relationships to one another and to the planet.

The insights gained from speculative YA fiction about possibilities for the future can also illuminate the past. If we look back at the YA ur-text, *The Outsiders*, for example, keeping in mind the ideas about cosmopolitan reading, local allegiances, and climate, the novel shifts slightly. The attempts made by members of both the Greasers and the Socs to reach outside their groups toward one another suggest the need for—and difficulty of making such connections: Cherry Valence, a Soc, tells the police that the Greaser who killed a Soc did so only because the Soc was trying to drown his friend. Because Cherry refuses to maintain the official story that positions the Socs as the good guys and the Greasers as thugs, Ponyboy starts to shift his thinking about his local monsters. And although at this point the poem that Ponyboy's friend recites—Robert Frost's "Nothing Gold Can Stay"— has become a cliché, it nevertheless suggests the importance of texts and countertexts in the adolescent imaginary. We might also think about the environmental factors that shape an Oklahoma oil town, considering that many of the Greasers (including Ponyboy's brothers) have laboring jobs, including jobs at gas stations: They are "grease monkeys" who eke out a living at the consumer end of the oil production. The Oklahoma oil fields have led to Oklahoma being forty-first in the United States on a list of state environmental health, a position worsened by ongoing drought (a 2021 farm report indicates that more than 90% of the state is "abnormally dry").

And as an incredibly powerful iteration of reading with multiple stories in mind, we might consider the violence between the Greasers and the Socs as a continuation of Tulsa's violent legacy, a history that many would like to ban from high school curricula: the 1921 Greenwood Massacre, when white rioters destroyed the section of Tulsa known as Black Wall Street, an affluent African American neighborhood. Hundreds were killed, thousands of homes were burned, and no charges were ever filed. The community rebuilt itself, only to be devastated again, several years after the publication of *The Outsiders*, when State and federal governments used eminent domain to seize property—owned primarily by African Americans—in order to build a major highway through the community's center. When we know "the context of stuff," as Sunny says, we see more layers in *The Outsiders*, and we also see the ways in which YA can open up the space for conversations—about history, about resources, about structures of community and engagement.

Given that so much of YA fiction asks its readers to question their local allegiances, it is perhaps unsurprising that YA books so often end up on lists of banned books. And yet as intolerance and xenophobia seem to be on the rise around the world and as the United States, in particular, seems intent on trying to suppress or ignore its racist history in favor of a nationalist narrative that extols American exceptionalism, it seems more important than ever to pay attention to the cultural work of YA literature. If books are banned from school libraries and bookstores, if websites are censored, and so on, how can anyone learn "the context of stuff"? As Viet Thanh Nguyen wrote in *The New York Times*, "banning is an act of fear—the fear of dangerous and contagious ideas. The best, and perhaps most dangerous, books deliver these ideas in something just as troubling and infectious: a good story" (np). Good stories imbue us with wonder and wonder can be an antidote to fear: When Sunny sees a downed Biafran fighter jet in a magical jungle, for instance, "her first reaction wasn't fear or horror, it was wonder" (*Akata Woman*, 260). When we engage with wonder, we are able to stand outside of ourselves and see how we are connected to larger patterns in the world. Both irony and wonder require the ability to think and respond on multiple levels, to engage with multiple narratives without insisting that any single narrative take priority. In an interview about his novel *The Overstory*, Richard Powers addresses the necessity of wonder:

> Awe and wonder are the first, most basic tools involved in turning toward and becoming attentive to … meaning above and beyond our own … . This is what I'd ask the critics of the literature of extra-human awe: Which is more childish, naïve, romantic, or mystical: the belief that we can get away with making Earth revolve around our personal appetites and fantasies, or the belief that a vast, multi-million-pronged project four and a half billion years old deserves a little reverent humility?
>
> (Hamner np)

This sense of "reverent humility" could be seen as a return to ancient spiritual practices that respond to the planet as a sentient being. And yet, as these novels demonstrate, we are long past the moment of being able to return to some primordial innocent past; we are enmeshed in the webs of our own destruction.

At the end of *Akata Woman*, the Covid-19 crisis is just beginning and Sunny is full of apprehension about what will happen, as we all were, in the winter of 2020. Aba and the rest of the world are retreating into lockdown, an enactment of precisely what Steffen warns us against: acting as if we could isolate ourselves from someone else's crisis.

Sunny asks Udide if she could "weave the virus away," hoping, that is, for some kind of magical resolution. The spider deity tells Sunny that the virus isn't her business and that "humanity will see this through, or it will not" (*Woman* 393). Udide does acknowledge that given what's happening in the world, "it's good that I now have all my tools." These tools include the ghazal that Sunny returned to her, which suggests the necessity of creative work to "see this through." The creative leaps of engagement made by YA literature function like our own ghazals, offering us the tools we need to see ourselves through, to create the conversations we need in order to challenge the behaviors that have brought us to the brink of oblivion.

We need this speculative YA fiction to help us imagine "what if": What if we found new stories or new strength in old stories; what if the world no longer needed national boundaries; what if there were non-metaphorical monsters in our midst? Speculative fiction, Margaret Atwood tells us, "explore[s] the nature and limits of what it means to be human in very explicit ways, by pushing the human envelope as far as it can go in the direction of the not-quite-human [and] help[ing] us to understand and navigate differences" (60). To read with wonder, to consider the boundaries and limitations of our own human experience, helps us to "explore a wider range of possibilities for living," as Nalo Hopkinson says about her work (Johnston 203). YA speculative fiction, like YA fiction in general, opens conversations about the shape of the world and invites nonspecialized readers into discussions about public policy, identity, agency, nation, and the fate of the planet. We need these books because they reflect ourselves back to ourselves and, in so doing, give us new ways to see the world.

Works Cited

"Ending Violence Against Native Women" | Indian Law Resource Center. Accessed January 31, 2022. https://indianlaw.org/issue/ending-violence-against-native-women.

Adebayo, Bukola. "Major New Inquiry into Oil Spills in Nigeria's Niger Delta Launched." *CNN*, March 27, 2019. https://edition.cnn.com/2019/03/26/africa/nigeria-oil-spill-inquiry-intl/index.html.

Adichie, Chimamanda Ngozi. "The Danger of a Single Story." TED Talk, October 7, 2009. https://www.youtube.com/watch?v=D9Ihs241zeg.

Adoni, Hanna, and Hillel Nossek. "The Cultural Divide: Book Reading as a Signifier of Boundaries among Co-Cultures in Israeli Society." *Israel Studies Review* 28, no. 1 (2013): 54–77.

Alter, Alexandra. "Nnedi Okorafor and the Fantasy Genre She Is Helping Redefine." *The New York Times*, October 6, 2017, sec. Books. https://www.nytimes.com/2017/10/06/books/ya-fantasy-diverse-akata-warrior.html.

Anker, Elizabeth S., and Rita Felski. *Critique and Postcritique*. Duke University Press, 2017.

Anzaldúa, Gloria. *Borderlands / La Frontera*. (1987) Aunt Lute Books, 2012.

Appiah, Kwame Anthony. "Cosmopolitan Patriots." *Critical Inquiry* 23, no. 3 (1997): 617–639.

Appiah, Kwame Anthony. "Rooted Cosmopolitanism." In *The Ethics of Identity*, 213–272. Princeton University Press, 2005. https://doi.org/10.2307/j.ctt7t9f0.9.

Appiah, Kwame Anthony. *Cosmopolitanism: Ethics in a World of Strangers*. WW Norton, 2006.

Arac, Jonathan, and Holly Yanacek. "Keywords, Structures of Feeling, and the Novel." *Novel* 54, no. 1 (May 1, 2021): 121–129. https://doi.org/10.1215/00295132-8868869.

Ardeneaux, Edward, IV. "SF's Revolutionary Imagination: Hacking Beyond Neoliberalism in Daniel Suarez's Daemon and Freedom^{TM} and G. Willow Wilson's Alif the Unseen." *Journal of the Fantastic in the Arts* 30, no. 3 (2019): 373–391.

Association of American Publishers. "Book Publisher Revenue Estimated at $25.8 Billion in 2018." June 21, 2019. https://publishers.org/news/book-publisher-revenue-estimated-at-25-8-billion-in-2018/.

Atwood, Margaret. *In Other Worlds: SF and the Human Imagination*. Anchor, 2011.

Braidotti, Rosi. *Nomadic Subjects: Embodiment and Sexual Difference in Contemporary Feminist Theory*. Columbia University Press, 2011.

Braidotti, Rosi. *Nomadic Theory: The Portable Rosi Braidotti*. Columbia University Press, 2011.

Braidotti, Rosi. "Becoming-world." *After Cosmopolitanism*, edited by Rosi Braidotti et al., 29–66. Routledge, 2012.

Breckenridge, Carol A., et al. *Cosmopolitanism*. Duke University Press, 2002.

Bundel, Ani. "Is Dumbledore gay? Why JK Rowling's continual character revisionism is getting old." March 24, 2019. https://www.nbcnews.com/think/opinion/dumbledore-gay-why-j-k-rowling-s-continual-character-revisionism-ncna986726.

Butler, Octavia E. *Parable of the Sower*. (1993) Open Road Media, 2012.

Butler, Octavia E. *Parable of the Talents*. (1998) Open Road Media, 2012.

Buurma, Rachel Sagner, and Laura Heffernan. "The Common Reader and the Archival Classroom: Disciplinary History for the Twenty-First Century." *New Literary History* 43, no. 1 (2012): 113–135.

Byatt, A. S. "Harry Potter and the Childish Adult." *The New York Times*, July 7, 2003, sec. Opinion. https://www.nytimes.com/2003/07/07/opinion/harry-potter-and-the-childish-adult.html.

Cantrell, Sarah K. "Letting Specters In: Environmental Catastrophe and the Limits of Space in Philip Pullman's *His Dark Materials*." *Children's Literature Association Quarterly*, 39, no. 2 (Summer 2014): 234–251.

Cart, Michael. "The Value of Young Adult Literature" | Young Adult Library Services Association (YALSA). Accessed December 11, 2021. https://www.ala.org/yalsa/guidelines/whitepapers/yalit.

Coates, Tyler. "J.K. Rowling Wants You to Know How Gay Dumbledore Really Was." *Esquire*, March 18, 2019. https://www.esquire.com/entertainment/books/a26858267/j-k-rowling-dumbledore-grindelwald-gay-harry-potter/.

Cohen, Jeffrey Jerome. *Monster Theory: Reading Culture*. University of Minnesota Press, 1996.

Coleman, Christian. "Interview with Rebecca Roanhorse," *Lightspeed Magazine*, April 2019. https://www.lightspeedmagazine.com/nonfiction/interview-rebecca-roanhorse/.

Damrosch, David. *What Is World Literature?* Princeton University Press, 2003.

Damrosch, David. *How to Read World Literature*. John Wiley & Sons, 2017.

Dharwadker, Vinay. *Cosmopolitan Geographies: New Locations in Literature and Culture*. Routledge, 2001.

Eccleshare, Julia. "What to Read to Younger Children When Harry Potter Gets Too Dark." *The Guardian*, May 3, 2016. https://www.theguardian.com/childrens-books-site/2016/may/03/harry-potter-jk-rowling-what-to-read-when-too-dark.

Edwards, Brian T. *After the American Century*. Columbia University Press, 2016.

Egbunike, Louisa Uchum. "Re-Presenting Africa in Young Adult Speculative Fiction: The Ekpe Institution in Nnedi Okorafor's *Akata Witch*." *ALT 33*

Children's Literature & Story-Telling: African Literature Today, edited by Ernest N. Emenyonu, 141–155. Boydell & Brewer, 2015.

Ennis, Dawn. "JK Rowling Comes Out As a TERF," *Forbes*, Dec 19, 2019. https://www.forbes.com/sites/dawnstaceyennis/2019/12/19/jk-rowling-comes-out-as-a-terf/?sh=ea2444c5d70e.

Falconer, Rachel. *The Crossover Novel: Contemporary Children's Fiction and Its Adult Readership*. Routledge, 2009.

Farmer, Nancy. *House of Scorpion*. Simon & Schuster, 2002.

Farmer, Nancy. *Lord of Opium*. Simon & Schuster, 2013.

Felski, Rita. *Hooked: Art and Attachment*. University of Chicago Press, 2020.

Fitzsimmons, Rebekah. "Testing the Tastemakers: Children's Literature, Bestseller Lists, and the 'Harry Potter Effect.'" *Children's Literature* 40, no. 1 (2012): 78–107. https://doi.org/10.1353/chl.2012.0002.

Flood, Alison. "The Rise of BookTok: Meet the Teen Influencers Pushing Books up the Charts." *The Guardian*, June 25, 2021. https://www.theguardian.com/books/2021/jun/25/the-rise-of-booktok-meet-the-teen-influencers-pushing-books-up-the-charts.

Friedman, Susan Stanford. "Translational Migrations: Novel Homelands in Monica Ali's *Brick Lane*." In *Times of Mobility: Transnational Literature and Gender in Translation*, edited by Jasmina Lukíc, Sibelan Forrester, and Borbála Faragó, 1st ed., 1: 19–46. Central European University Press, 2019. http://www.jstor.org/stable/10.7829/j.ctvzsmdm4.5.

Ghosh, Amitav. *The Great Derangement: Climate Change and the Unthinkable*. University of Chicago Press, 2016.

Graham, Ruth. "Against YA." *Slate*, June 5, 2014. https://slate.com/culture/2014/06/against-ya-adults-should-be-embarrassed-to-read-childrens-books.html.

Gruner, Elisabeth Rose. *Constructing the Adolescent Reader in Contemporary Young Adult Fiction*. Palgrave Macmillan, 2019.

Hamner, Everett. "Here's to Unsuicide: An Interview with Richard Powers." *Los Angeles Review of Books*, April 7, 2018. https://lareviewofbooks.org/article/heres-to-unsuicide-an-interview-with-richard-powers/.

Haraway, Donna. "Science, Technology, and Socialist-Feminism in the Late Twentieth Century," in *Simians, Cyborgs and Women: The Reinvention of Nature*, 149–181. Routledge, 1991.

Haraway, Donna. "Anthropocene, Capitalocene, Plantationocene, Chthulucene: Making Kin." *Environmental Humanities* 6 (2015): 159–165.

Harrison, Jennifer. *Posthumanist Readings in Dystopian Young Adult Fiction: Negotiating The Nature/Culture Divide*. Lexington Books, 2019.

Heise, Ursula K. *Sense of Place and Sense of Planet: The Environmental Imagination of the Global*. Oxford University Press, 2008.

Hollinger, David A. "From Identity to Solidarity." *Daedalus*, 135, no. 4 (2006): 23–31.

Hopkinson, Nalo. *Brown Girl in the Ring*. Warner Books, 1998.

Hopkinson, Nalo, editor. *So Long Been Dreaming: Postcolonial Science Fiction and Fantasy*. Arsenal Pulp Press, 2004.

Jaques, Zoe. *Children's Literature and the Posthuman: Animal, Environment, Cyborg*. Taylor & Francis Group, 2014.

Johnston, Nancy. "Happy That It's Here: An Interview with Nalo Hopkinson." In *Queer Universes: Sexualities in Science Fiction*, edited by Wendy Gay Pearson et al, 200–215. Liverpool University Press, 2008.

Kakutani, Michiko. "An Epic Showdown as Harry Potter Is Initiated Into Adulthood." *The New York Times*, July 19, 2007. https://www.nytimes.com/2007/07/19/books/19potter.html.

Kimmerer, Robin. "Speaking of Nature." *Orion Magazine*, 2017. https://orionmagazine.org:443/article/speaking-of-nature/.

Kitchener, Caroline. "Why So Many Adults Read Young-Adult Literature." *The Atlantic*, December 1, 2017. https://www.theatlantic.com/entertainment/archive/2017/12/why-so-many-adults-are-love-young-adult-literature/547334/.

Lathey, Gillian. "The Travels of Harry: International Marketing and the Translation of J. K. Rowling's *Harry Potter* Books." *The Lion and the Unicorn* 29, no. 2 (2005): 141–151.

Levin, Dan. "In a World 'So Upside Down,' the Virus Is Taking a Toll on Young People's Mental Health." *The New York Times*, May 20, 2020. https://www.nytimes.com/2020/05/20/us/coronavirus-young-people-emotional-toll.html?searchResultPosition=7.

McCulloch, Fiona. *Contemporary British Children's Fiction and Cosmopolitanism*. Taylor & Francis Group, 2016.

Mental Health America. "2020 Mental Health in America – Youth Data" https://www.mhanational.org/issues/2020/mental-health-america-youth-data.

Miller, Claire Cain. "How Other Nations Pay for Child Care. The U.S. Is an Outlier." *The New York Times*, October 6, 2021. https://www.nytimes.com/2021/10/06/upshot/child-care-biden.html.

Mustola, Marleena, and Sanna Karkulehto, "Wild Things Squeezed in the Closet: Monsters of Children's Literature as Nonhuman Others." In *Reconfiguring Human, Nonhuman and Posthuman in Literature and Culture*, edited by Sanna Karkulehto, Aino-Kaisa Koistinen, and Essi Varis, 125–142. Taylor & Francis Group, 2019.

The National. "G Willow Wilson Makes the Magical Come Alive in *Alif the Unseen*." Accessed October 17, 2021. https://www.thenationalnews.com/arts-culture/books/g-willow-wilson-makes-the-magical-come-alive-in-alif-the-unseen-1.443117.

National Congress of American Indians. "Demographics." June 1, 2020. https://www.ncai.org/about-tribes/demographics.

Nelson, Alondra. "Making the Impossible Possible: An Interview with Nalo Hopkinson." *Social Text* 20, no. 2 (2002): 97–113.

Newcomb, Erin T. "The Soul of the Clone: Coming of Age as a Posthuman in Nancy Farmer's *The House of the Scorpion*." In *Contemporary Dystopian Fiction for Young Adults: Brave New Teenagers*, edited by Carrie Hintz et al., 175–188. Routledge, 2013.

Nguyen, Viet Thanh. "My Young Mind Was Disturbed by a Book. It Changed My Life." *The New York Times*, January 29, 2022. https://www.nytimes.com/2022/01/29/opinion/culture/book-banning-viet-thanh-nguyen.html.

Nixon, Rob. *Slow Violence and the Environmentalism of the Poor*. Harvard University Press, 2011.

Nussbaum, Martha. "Liberal Education and Global Community." *Liberal Education* 90, no. 1 (Winter 2004): 42–47.

Oklahoma Farm Report. http://www.oklahomafarmreport.com/wire/news/2021/12/00287_DroughtMonitor12092021_124236.php#.Yh9DohNBx6o.

Okorafor, Nnedi. *Akata Witch*. Viking Penguin, 2011.

Okorafor, Nnedi. "Sci-fi Stories That Imagine a Future Africa." TED Global, August 2017. https://www.ted.com/talks/nnedi_okorafor_sci_fi_stories_that_imagine_a_future_africa?language=en.

Okorafor, Nnedi. *Akata Warrior*. Viking Penguin, 2017.

Okorafor, Nnedi. *Akata Woman*. Viking Penguin, 2022.

Price, Gary. "NPD Reports, '2021 is Shaping Up to be a Very Good Year for Young Adult Fiction.'" *InfoDocket Library Journal*, May 25, 2021. https://www.infodocket.com/2021/05/25/npd-reports-2021-is-shaping-up-to-be-a-very-good-year-for-young-adult-fiction/#:~:text=The%20young%2Dadult%20fiction%20category,according%20to%20The%20NPD%20Group.

Ramuglia, River. "Cli-fi, Petroculture, and the Environmental Humanities: An Interview with Stephanie LeMenager." *Studies in the Novel*, 50, no. 1 (Spring 2018): 154–164.

Rivera, Lysa. "Neoliberalism and Dystopia in U.S.–Mexico Borderlands Fiction." In *Blast, Corrupt, Dismantle, Erase: Contemporary North American Dystopian Literature*, edited by Gisèle Marie Baxter, Brett Josef Brubisic, and Tara Lee, 291–311. Wilfrid Laurier University Press, 2014.

Roanhorse, Rebecca. *Trail of Lightning*. Gallery/Saga Press, 2018.

Roanhorse, Rebecca. "Interview." *Tor*. May 7, 2019 https://www.tor.com/2019/05/07/rebecca-roanhorse-reddit-ama-storm-of-locusts-trail-of-lightning/.

Roanhorse, Rebecca. *Storm of Locusts*. Gallery/Saga Press, 2019.

Romano, Aja. "Harry Potter and the Author Who Failed Us." *Vox*, June 11, 2020. https://www.vox.com/culture/21285396/jk-rowling-transphobic-backlash-harry-potter.

Rowling, J. K. *Harry Potter and the Sorcerer's Stone*. Scholastic Press, 1998.

Rowling, J. K. *Harry Potter and the Chamber of Secrets*. Scholastic Press, 1999.

Rowling, J. K. *Harry Potter and the Prisoner of Azkaban*. Scholastic Press, 1999.

Rowling, J. K. *Harry Potter and the Goblet of Fire*. Scholastic Press, 2000.

Rowling, J. K. *Harry Potter and the Order of the Phoenix*. Scholastic Press, 2003.

Rowling, J. K. *Harry Potter and the Half-Blood Prince*. Scholastic Press, 2005.

Rowling, J. K. *Harry Potter and the Deathly Hallows*. Scholastic Press, 2007.

Rowling, J. K. "Statement from J. K. Rowling Regarding the Robert F Kennedy Human Rights Ripple of Hope Award." Accessed January 13, 2022. https://www.jkrowling.com/opinions/statement-from-j-k-rowling-regarding-the-robert-f-kennedy-human-rights-ripple-of-hope-award/.

Rowling, J. K. "JK Rowling Writes About Her Reasons for Speaking Out on Sex and Gender Issues." August 27, 2020. Accessed June 10, 2020.

Rutledge, Gregory E. "Speaking in Tongues: An Interview with Science Fiction Writer Nalo Hopkinson." *African American Review* 33, no. 4 (1999): 589–601. https://doi.org/10.2307/2901339.

Rylance, Rick. *Literature and the Public Good*. Oxford University Press, 2016.

Saunders, John H., Michael Warren Tumolo, Jennifer Beidendorf, Mary Elizabeth Bezanson, Lauren Rose Camacci, Joshua D. Hill, Lauren Lemley, Brett Lunceford, Deborah Lee Norland, and Christopher J. Oldenburg. *The Rhetorical Power of Children's Literature*. Lexington Books, 2016.

Schoefer, Christine. "Harry Potter's Girl Trouble." *Salon*, January 13, 2000. https://www.salon.com/2000/01/13/potter/.

Sheldrake, Merlin. *Entangled Life: How Fungi Make Our Worlds, Change Our Minds and Shape Our Futures*. Random House, 2020.

Simpson, David. "Raymond Williams: Feeling for Structures, Voicing 'History.'" *Social Text* 30 (1992): 9–26. https://doi.org/10.2307/466464.

Slaughter, John R. "Only Reading: An Introduction." *ELH* 80, no. 2 (Summer 2013): 317–321.

Sombatpoonsiri, Janjira. "From Repression to Revolt: Thailand's 2020 Protests and the Regional Implications." German Institute of Global and Area Studies (GIGA), 2021. http://www.jstor.org/stable/resrep30227.

Stamets, Paul. "How Mushrooms Can Clean Up Radioactive Contamination – An 8 Step Plan." https://www.permaculture.co.uk/articles/how-mushrooms-can-clean-radioactive-contamination-8-step-plan.

Steffen, Alex. "The Transapocalyptic Now." Substack newsletter. *The Snap Forward* (blog), November 5, 2021. https://alexsteffen.substack.com/p/the-transapocalyptic-now.

Steffen, Alex. "We're Not yet Ready for What's Already Happened." Substack newsletter. *The Snap Forward* (blog), May 19, 2021. https://alexsteffen.substack.com/p/were-not-yet-ready-for-whats-already.

Stein, Rachel. "Bodily Invasions: Gene Trading and Organ Theft in Octavia Butler and Nalo Hopkinson's Speculative Fiction." In *New Perspectives on Environmental Justice: Gender, Sexuality, and Activism*, edited by Rachel Stein et al., 209–224. Rutgers University Press, 2004.

Sutherland, John. "Republic of Letters: Literature Without Borders." In *A Little History of Literature*, 241–247. Yale University Press, 2013. http://www.jstor.org/stable/j.ctt5vkwh2.39.

Tarr, Anita, and Donna R. White, editors. *Posthumanism in Young Adult Fiction Finding Humanity in a Posthuman World*. University Press of Mississippi, 2018. http://proxy.library.nyu.edu/login?url=https://muse.jhu.edu/book/60652.

Tatar, Maria. *The Heroine with 1001 Faces*. WW Norton, 2021.

Teare, Elizabeth. "Harry Potter and the Technology of Magic." In *Ivory Tower and Harry Potter: Perspectives on a Literary Phenomenon*, edited by Lana A. Whited, 329–342. University of Missouri Press, 2002.

Thiel, Liz, and Alison Waller. "Introduction." *Bookbird* 50, no. 3 (2012): 3–7.

Thomas, Ebony Elizabeth. *The Dark Fantastic: Race and the Imagination from Harry Potter to the Hunger Games*. University Press, 2019.

Tsing, Anna Lowenhaupt. *The Mushroom at the End of the World: On the Possibility of Life in Capitalist Ruins*. Princeton University Press, 2015.

Turner, Bryan S. "Cosmopolitan Virtue, Globalization and Patriotism." *Theory, Culture & Society* 19, nos. 1–2 (2002): 45–63.

Walkowitz, Rebecca. *Born Translated: The Contemporary Novel in an Age of World Literature*. Columbia University Press, 2015.

Warner, Marina. *Stranger Magic: Charmed States and the Arabian Nights*. Belknap Press of Harvard University Press, 2012.

Williams, Deborah Lindsay. "Witches, Monsters, and Questions of Nation: Humans and Non-Humans in *Akata Witch* and *Trail of Lightning*." *International Journal of Young Adult Literature* 1, no. 1 (2020): 1–19.

Williams, Raymond. *Preface to a Film*. Film Drama Limited, 1954.

Williams, Raymond. *Marxism and Literature*. Oxford University Press, 1977.

Wilson, G. Willow. *Alif the Unseen*. Grove Press, 2012.

Woodward, Will. "Harry Potter Books Are Sexist, Says US Academic." *The Guardian*, January 10, 2001. https://www.theguardian.com/uk/2001/jan/10/books.education.

Zhong, Raymond. "These Climate Scientists Are Fed Up and Ready to Go On Strike." *The New York Times*, March 1, 2022. https://www.nytimes.com/2022/03/01/climate/ipcc-climate-scientists-strike.html.

Zipes, Jack. *Sticks and Stones: The Troublesome Success of Children's Literature from Slovenly Peter to Harry Potter*. Routledge, 2001.

Index